ARE YOU
LISTENING?

NICK FAWCETT

ARE YOU LISTENING?

HONEST

PRAYERS

ABOUT

LIFE

kevin
mayhew

First published in 1998.
This edition published in 2004 by

KEVIN MAYHEW LTD
Buxhall, Stowmarket, Suffolk, IP14 3BW
E-mail: info@kevinmayhewltd.com

KINGSGATE PUBLISHING INC
1000 Pannell Street, Suite G, Columbia, MO 65201
E-mail: sales@kingsgatepublishing.com

9 8 7 6 5 4 3 2 1 0

ISBN 1 84417 223 6
Catalogue No 1500696

Cover design by Angela Selfe
Edited by Katherine Laidler
Typesetting by Louise Selfe
Printed and bound in Great Britain

Dedication

To my wife Deborah,
with love and thanks for the help and support
which has made this book possible

About the author

Nick Fawcett was born in 1957. He studied Theology at Bristol University and Regent's Park College, Oxford. His early years of ministry were spent in Somerset and Lancashire, and from 1989 to 1996 he was Minister of Gas Green Baptist Church, Cheltenham. In 1996 he became Toc H's Chaplain and Development Officer for Wales and the West of England.

He continues to work part-time for Toc H but is now devoting more time to freelance work as a proof-reader and indexer, and particularly to writing. He is the author of *No Ordinary Man,* Books 1 and 2 (1997, 2000), *Prayers For All Seasons,* Books 1 and 2 (1998, 2001), *Getting It Across,* Books 1 and 2 (1999, 2003), *The Unfolding Story* (2000), *To Put It Another Way* (2000), *A Quiet Word* (2001) and *Daily Prayer* (2001), all published by Kevin Mayhew Publishers.

He is married to Deborah and they have two young children, Samuel and Katie.

Contents

Introduction

Do you find prayer easy? I don't. Though I have led prayer in worship for many years, when it comes to talking directly to God I often find myself struggling for words. And, through my experience as a minister, I know that many feel the same. Whilst at times, for us all, prayer can be a huge blessing, at others it can become little more than a duty, even a chore.

So why? Well, perhaps one reason is that we make prayer too formal. There is nothing wrong with that in the context of public worship – indeed there it is probably necessary, but when it comes to personal devotion it's different. Prayer is meant to be the expression of a relationship, not an exercise in composition or grammar, and that should mean we feel able to be honest to God, free to bring before him the things that matter to us, the good and the bad, the joys and the sorrows, the hopes and the fears. That's what this collection of prayers aims to help us do. It starts from daily life and brings before God the emotions which are part of it – fear, hope, joy, sorrow, excitement, anxiety, and countless others. Each is offered openly to him.

But, of course, prayer doesn't end with us, or at least it shouldn't do. It is meant to be about dialogue – here perhaps is another reason some of us struggle with it, because it can all too often seem anything but. We may speak glibly about prayer being a conversation – even, as one children's chorus puts it, like a telephone – but in reality it's not. We've all had times when we pour out our souls and it's like staring into a black hole, when we cry out for an answer and find only silence, when we look for guidance but find none forthcoming. Yet it may be that the answer is there more often than we might think, if only we know where to look – and where better than in the Scriptures? So often, when we turn to the Bible, it is as if to find words written expressly for us, offering the answer we are looking for, the message we so urgently need to hear. It is this that lies behind the second part of each prayer in this collection. I do not presume in any way to set myself up as God, but rather to make suggestions, based upon Bible passages, which may open the way to understanding what God would say to us.

All the material in this book is written primarily for use in personal devotion, though some could effectively be used in public worship, one person reading the first part of each prayer, and another the second. Everything I have written is inevitably coloured by my own ideas and experiences, but it is also a reflection of the joys and sorrows, the hopes and inspirations of so many I have been privileged to know during the course of my ministry. I hope it may also be a reflection of life for you, and some help in leading to a deeper and more personal encounter with God.

Nick Fawcett

1

It's me, O Lord

What sort of language should we use in prayer? What sort of subjects are appropriate to bring before God? Most of us would probably find questions like these hard to answer, for our response would almost certainly depend on what we were praying for and how we were feeling at the time. Occasionally prayer simply flows, our innermost feelings finding expression naturally and spontaneously. But there are times also when we approach prayer almost mechanically, saying what we think God wants to hear rather than what we really want to tell him. Why? Partly, I think, because there lurks in many of us a vague sense that prayer requires a special sort of language, almost a technical expertise, if God is to hear us. But perhaps the main reason is that we feel some matters are best kept to ourselves. Yet if prayer is to nurture our faith and our growth as individuals, to become a dialogue rather than a monologue, we need to be honest with God and bring ourselves as we are with no holds barred.

Two men went up to the temple to pray, one a Pharisee and the other a tax collector. The Pharisee, standing by himself, was praying thus, 'God, I thank you that I am not like

other people: thieves, rogues, adulterers, or
even like this tax collector. I fast twice a week;
I give a tenth of all my income.' But the tax
collector, standing far off, would not even look
up to heaven, but was beating his breast and
saying, 'God, be merciful to me, a sinner!'
Luke 18:10-13

Simon Peter fell down at Jesus' knees, saying,
'Go away from me, Lord, for I am a sinful man!'
Luke 5:8

It's me, O Lord:
  not the person I pretend to be,
  nor who I want to be,
  but me, as I am,
  with all my strengths,
  all my weaknesses,
  all my faith,
  all my doubt –
  me, as I've rarely dared come before,
  reaching out to you in prayer.
I've no right to be here, I know that,
  for I'm nothing special,
  nothing to write home about,
  and I've little idea what I'm going to say,
  still less how to say it.
But you tell us if we truly seek, we shall find,
  if we're really sorry, you'll forgive,
  if we keep on asking, you will answer.

So I'm here, Lord,
   in all my ugliness and sin –
   weak,
   selfish,
   greedy,
   thoughtless –
   but I'm here,
   and I'm asking you, despite it all:
   hear my prayer.

My child,
   don't stop,
   keep talking,
   for I'm here too,
   delighted to listen,
   drinking in your every word.
It's a joy to hear you, believe me,
   music to my ears –
   no need to apologise or excuse yourself.
I've looked forward to this moment for so long,
   your coming openly and honestly to meet me.
For it's *you* I want to talk to –
   not the mask you wear for the world;
   you as you really are –
   the face you show, the face you hide,
   the person you love, the person you hate.
They're both you,
   two halves of the same whole,
   inseparable as light and dark,
   substance and shadow,

and unless you bring all,
openly and honestly before me,
you bring nothing.
You're not perfect – I know that –
but I don't ask you to be;
it's not me who twists the knife, only yourself.
I love you as you are,
with all your faults and fragile faith,
and I'll go on loving you day after day,
drawing you closer to me
not as a condition but an expression of that love.
So come now, gladly and confidently,
bring yourself with head bent low
but soul held high,
and find in me your kindest critic
and truest friend.

*Ask, and it will be given to you; search, and you
will find; knock, and the door will be opened
for you. For everyone who asks receives, and
everyone who searches finds, and for everyone
who knocks, the door will be opened.*
Matthew 7:7-8

*If we say that we have no sin, we deceive
ourselves, and the truth is not in us. If we
confess our sins, he who is faithful and just will
forgive us our sins and cleanse us from all
unrighteousness.* 1 John 1:8-9

2

Lord, I can't carry on much longer!

For us all there are times when life gets on top of us – the pressures and demands too much to bear. And for most of us such moments are nearer than we might imagine, for who can say what tomorrow might bring? We may feel everything is under control, life running along smoothly, but it only takes one setback, one disappointment, to change our whole perspective, sending us spiralling into a vortex of chaos and confusion. Yet at the heart of our faith is the conviction that God is always there to support us, able to give us strength whatever we may face. And when we finally emerge from the darkness, it can be then to see the whole of life in a new light.

Save me, O God, for the waters have come up to my neck. I sink in deep mire, where there is no foothold; I have come into deep waters, and the flood sweeps over me. I am weary with my crying; my throat is parched. My eyes grow dim with waiting for my God. Psalm 69:1-3

Thus says the man: I am weary, O God, I am weary, O God. How can I prevail?
Proverbs 30:1

Lord, I can't carry on much longer!
Do you hear me?
I'm fraying at the edges,
    coming apart at the seams,
    and it's only a matter of time
    before I fall to pieces completely.
What's happened, Lord?
I thought I was in control,
    master of my own destiny,
    one of the few survivors
    in this rough old world of ours.
All right, I had my problems, I admit it –
    the nagging worries,
    the hidden fears,
    the pent-up emotions –
    but we all have those, don't we – all of us?
I'd learned to live with those over the years,
    even to welcome them in a funny way,
    for I felt knowing my weaknesses
    somehow gave me control.
But not any longer.
Suddenly the world's been turned upside down:
    everything I'd put my trust in –
    so solid and certain – all at once so insecure.
And now I'm on the edge of a precipice,
    hanging on by my fingertips,
    a deep, dark cavern opening up beneath me.
I'm slipping, Lord!
I'm falling!
Are you listening?
Help!

My child,
> you *can* carry on, believe me.

You may not think so,
> but you have the resources to keep going,
> or do you really think
> that I'd have brought you this far
> simply to abandon you now?

Of course not!

I'm with you always,
> in the good and the bad,
> the pleasure and the pain,
> the joy and the sorrow.

Whether you see me or whether you don't,
> I'm there beside you,
> watching over you with a love
> that will never let you go.

But I can't do it all, tempting though it is,
> for that would be no help
> to either of us in the long run.

You may not welcome the hard times,
> but they're as necessary as any,
> for there can be no light without darkness,
> no laughter without tears,
> no beauty without ugliness,
> no life without death.

I'm afraid that's the way it has to be.

But when you finally reach the end of the tunnel,
> as you surely will,
> it will be to find your faith deeper,
> and yourself stronger,
> than you've ever dared to dream.

God is our refuge and our strength, a very present help in trouble. Therefore we will not fear, though the earth should change, though the mountains shake in the heart of the sea; though its waters roar and foam, though the mountains tremble with its tumult.

Psalm 46:1-3

We are afflicted in every way, but not crushed; perplexed, but not driven to despair; persecuted, but not forsaken; struck down, but not destroyed; always carrying in the body the death of Jesus, so that the life of Jesus may also be made visible in our bodies.

2 Corinthians 4:8-10

3

Why did I do it?

How often have you tried to turn over a new leaf, only to fall back into your old ways before you know it? How often have you made a new year's resolution, only to break it before the first day is out? As the old saying has it, 'The spirit is willing but the flesh is weak'. Try as we might, sometimes we just can't seem to help ourselves – temptation is too strong to resist. And it's easy at such times to lose heart or succumb to feelings of guilt. Yet we should never despair, for God is far less critical of us than we are of ourselves. He's grieved by our mistakes, of course, but, unlike us, he is always ready to forgive and forget, always ready to wipe the slate clean and help us begin again.

Have mercy on me, O God, according to your steadfast love; according to your abundant mercy blot out my transgressions. Wash me thoroughly from my iniquity, and cleanse me from my sin. For I know my transgressions, and my sin is ever before me. Against you, you alone, have I sinned, and done what is evil in your sight, so that you are justified in your sentence and blameless when you pass judgement.
Psalm 51:1-4

For your name's sake, O Lord, pardon my guilt, for it is great. Psalm 25:11

I do not understand my own actions. For I do not do what I want, but I do the very thing I hate. I find it to be a law that when I want to do what is good, evil lies close at hand.
Romans 7:15, 21

Why did I do it, Lord?
Why did I let you down again?
After all those promises,
    all those resolutions,
    why is it I rush towards temptation
    like a moth attracted to a candle?
I cannot seem to help it.
Time and again I tell myself,
    'This time will be different! This time I will not fail!'
But when the moment comes
    it's the same old story –
    I resist for a moment,
    a token gesture,
    but in my heart I know it won't be long
    before the excuses win the day,
    and I give in yet again.
Why Lord?
Why am I so weak and foolish,
    unable even to live up to my own expectations,
    let alone yours?
Lord, I'm ashamed,

ashamed of what I do and who I am,
of having to come once more
asking for your forgiveness
when I have no right to expect it.
Forgive me.

My child, don't lose heart.
You did let me down, yes,
   and of course I'm disappointed,
   but I understand –
   I know what's going on deep inside you,
   and I realise you'd like to be different
   even if you never quite succeed.
Keep trying, always,
   no matter how many times you fail,
   or how often you feel like giving up –
   that's all I ask.
You'll still make mistakes,
   never be perfect,
   probably go on letting me down
   until your dying day –
   I realise that.
But, believe me, I won't be half as hard on you
   as you are on yourself.
I may be disappointed,
   but as long as you're truly sorry,
   I'll always be ready to forgive,
   and always ready to start again.
It's when you're no longer ashamed,
   when you don't care any more,

when your mistakes don't seem to matter –
it's then that I'll really start to worry,
and then perhaps you should start worrying too.

Happy are those whose transgression is for-given, whose sin is covered. Happy are those to whom the Lord imputes no iniquity, and in whose spirit there is no deceit. While I kept silence, my body wasted away through my groaning all day long. For day and night your hand was heavy upon me; my strength was dried up as by the heat of summer. Then I acknowledged my sin to you, and I did not hide my iniquity; I said, 'I will confess my transgressions to the Lord,' and you forgave the guilt of my sin. Psalm 32:1-5

No one who conceals transgressions will pros-per, but one who confesses and forsakes them will obtain mercy. Proverbs 28:13

Wretched man that I am! Who will rescue me from this body of death? Thanks be to God through Jesus Christ our Lord!
Romans 7:24-25

4

Lord, I woke up this morning

When I left the pastoral ministry to join the chaplaincy team of Toc H there was a price to pay – early mornings! With an area to cover stretching from Penzance to the Lake District, you can well imagine that there were times when an early start was called for, and for me that was a shock to the system! Mornings are not my favourite time, and I suspect many would say the same. We may occasionally greet the new day with a song in our hearts, but probably more often it is with a groan of dismay, the pressures and responsibilities of daily life weighing so heavily upon us that we wake with a sense of foreboding rather than anticipation. Yet every morning is God's gift, full of immeasurable potential and untold possibilities, if only we have eyes to see and ears to hear.

Satisfy us in the morning with your steadfast love, so that we may rejoice and be glad all our days. Psalm 90:14

Lord, I woke up this morning,
    the sun streaming in at the window,
    birds singing in the garden,
    a gentle breeze whispering in the trees –
    and I wanted to sing for joy,
    to shout your praise from the rooftops,
    for suddenly life was wonderful,
    a taste of Eden.
I looked round,
    at the clouds scudding in the sky,
    children walking to school,
    bees buzzing among the flowers,
    and the dew glistening on the grass –
    and I wondered how I could
    ever fail to notice these,
    how my eyes could be blind and my soul closed
    to the loveliness of life.
Yet it happens, Lord, all too often.
I wake up and feel pressure rather than promise,
    a sense of burden rather than blessing.
I get dressed,
    go to work,
    talk to friends,
    walk in the park,
    but though my eyes see all, my soul sees nothing,
    thoughts turned inwards instead of out,
    on my own little world
    instead of the world beyond.
But this morning was different,
    for you opened my eyes to the miracle of life
    and the beauty within it;

so I bring you my praise,
and offer this prayer:
teach me to *see*, Lord, new every morning.

My child,
   it's good to hear you,
   to witness your joy and glimpse your delight.
And, believe me,
   there's nothing I'd like better
   than to answer your prayer,
   to give you always what you feel this moment.
Yet I can't promise that,
   for I know through experience
   that what you see today you will miss tomorrow,
   and what speaks to you now may seem silent then.
It's not your fault,
   just the way of the world –
   your mind distracted by each day's passing cares.
Though the dawn will break and the sun still shine,
   though the birds will sing
   and the flowers still bloom,
   you may wake tomorrow and be blind to it all,
   unmoved by life's beauty,
   untouched by my presence.
But whether you see me, or whether you don't,
   whether morning brings joy, or fills you with dread,
   take heart, for I am with you,
   close by your side,
   from the dawn of the morning
   to the end of the day.

I will sing aloud of your steadfast love in the morning. For you have been a fortress for me and a refuge in the day of my distress. O my strength, I will sing praises to you, for you, O God, are my fortress, the God who shows me steadfast love. Psalm 59:16-17

The steadfast love of the Lord never ceases, his mercies never come to an end; they are new every morning; great is your faithfulness. 'The Lord is my portion,' says my soul, 'therefore I will hope in him.' Lamentations 3:22-24

5

God, I asked you this morning for patience

Patience, we are told, is a virtue, and I've no doubt that's right. It's also a very rare gift! Which of us hasn't stood waiting for the bus to arrive or the kettle to boil and cursed softly at the time it seems to be taking? All too easily we spend our lives racing around, one eye on the clock, begrudging every wasted moment. Yet the result is not only that others are made to suffer but that finally we do too, for, in our concern to save a few seconds here and there, we end up failing to appreciate all the time God has given us.

How long, O Lord? Will you forget me for ever? How long will you hide your face from me? How long must I bear pain in my soul, and have sorrow in my heart all day long? How long shall my enemy be exalted over me? Consider and answer me, O Lord my God!
Psalm 13:1-3a

As for me, is my complaint addressed to mortals? Why should I not be impatient?
Job 21:4

> *When they had come together, they asked him,*
> *'Lord, is this the time when you will restore the*
> *kingdom to Israel?' He replied, 'It is not for you*
> *to know the times or periods that the Father*
> *has set by his own authority.'*   Acts 1:6-7

God, I asked you this morning for patience,
   for help to take things more slowly,
   to stay cool,
   unflustered,
   in control.
But look what's happened.
I'm as bad as ever,
   worse if anything.
When the doctor's surgery was running
   a few minutes late
   I sat there fuming,
   and when the lights turned to red on the way home
   I could almost feel steam rising,
   as though my head must surely explode!
It's the same every time.
I don't mean to snap at anyone –
   I just can't help it.
I don't intend to complain –
   but before I know it the words are out
   and the damage is done.
What happened, Lord?
Weren't you listening?
Doesn't it matter to you?
Don't you care?

My child,
    I hear what you're saying, believe me,
    and I can see that you're doing your best.
But I'm afraid there's only one answer I can offer,
    and you're not going to like it,
    for it's what you've asked for,
    what you're so desperately seeking –
    patience!
That may sound nonsensical,
    but it's true,
    for I can't just give you patience,
    much as I'd like to.
It has to be cultivated,
    developed with time like everything else,
    and that means learning
    to live with all those situations
    which test your patience to the limit.
So when you feel the steam rising, ask yourself this:
    'What's the hurry?'
That job you're breaking your neck to finish,
    is it as important as you think?
The deadline you're trying so hard to meet,
    will it really not wait?
And those precious few seconds
    you're so desperate to save,
    will you ever fill them?
I doubt it.
If you could only pause for a moment and take stock,
    life would seem very different.
You may think you're saving time,
    but you're wasting it –

so concerned with the minutes you might lose,
you've lost sight of the hours you have.
Don't worry,
I heard your prayer this morning, loud and clear,
but to understand my answer you must realise this:
for patience to grow it must first be stretched!

*I waited patiently for the Lord; he inclined to
me and heard my cry.* Psalm 40:1

*Rejoice in hope, be patient in suffering, perse-
vere in prayer.* Romans 12:12

*Do not ignore this one fact, beloved, that with
the Lord one day is like a thousand years, and
a thousand years are like one day. The Lord is
not slow about his promise, as some think of
slowness, but is patient with you, not wanting
any to perish, but all to come to repentance.*
2 Peter 3:8-9

_ 6 _
I had it

Just occasionally life brings us a special, unforget-table moment which we wish we could preserve for ever, safe from the ravages of time. But, of course, we can't, and, if we try, it doesn't take long for what was sweet to turn *us* sour. Life moves on, and we must move with it. We cannot cling to the past and we should never try. If happiness is to be more than just the occasional fleeting moment, we must learn to let go and share it with others, instead of jealously guarding it as if it is our possession.

These things I remember, as I pour out my soul: how I went with the throng, and led them in procession to the house of God, with glad shouts and songs of thanksgiving, a multitude keeping festival. Psalm 42:4

When the Lord restored the fortunes of Zion, we were like those who dream. Then our mouth was filled with laughter, and our tongue with shouts of joy; then it was said among the nations, 'The Lord has done great things for them.' The Lord has done great things for us, and we rejoiced. Restore our fortunes, O Lord . . . May those who sow in tears reap with shouts of joy. Psalm 126:1-5

I had it, Lord –
    for a moment it was in my grasp,
    the happiness I've always dreamt of.
And I thought it was secure,
    locked carefully away,
    never again to elude me.
But it disappeared,
    here one minute, gone the next –
    like a butterfly dancing on the breeze,
    like a dream vanishing on waking,
    beautiful yet tantalising,
    full of promise yet failing to deliver.
What happened, Lord?
Did I let go?
Was I caught off guard?
Was my back turned?
I don't think so, for I was determined this time,
    resolved that, after all the disappointments,
    the burst bubbles,
    the false dreams,
    this time I would keep hold, come what may.
But it's gone, Lord,
    vanished without trace,
    and I'm begging you with aching heart:
    help me find it again.

My child,
I'm sorry, but you haven't understood.
You can't store happiness.
It's not something you can preserve or cling on to,

polishing it every so often
to keep the sparkle bright –
if you try that, you will surely lose it.
You must live one moment at a time,
celebrating it for what it is –
and then move on to the next.
You must take each day I give you,
rejoicing in what it brings –
and then let go.
If you want happiness to last
you must share it with others,
not hoard it away;
you must give it gladly,
not keep it to yourself.
That's when you'll find what you're looking for –
when you realise happiness isn't a possession
but a gift,
that life is not a destination but a journey.
You may wish you could stop the clock
and keep things as they are,
but you'd soon grow tired, believe me,
the precious jewel you think you hold
soon tarnished by familiarity.
So no more grieving,
no more regrets.
You imagine you've let something wonderful
slip from your grasp,
but you haven't;
you're still holding on, refusing to let go,
and that, I'm afraid, is the problem.

Those who go out weeping, bearing the seed for sowing, shall come home with shouts of joy, carrying their sheaves. Psalm 126:6

Do not store up for yourselves treasures on earth, where moth and rust consume and where thieves break in and steal; but store up for yourselves treasures in heaven . . . For where your treasure is, there your heart will be also.
Matthew 6:19-21

This is the day that the Lord has made; let us rejoice and be glad in it. Psalm 118:24

7

Lord, I'm not sure any more

To question something we once held dear is never easy, and when this involves a matter of faith it is doubly difficult. We feel that even the faintest suggestion of doubt is somehow a betrayal of God, and sadly there are always a few over-zealous individuals ready to reinforce such feelings. Yet, properly understood, doubt is a part of faith, almost its corollary. When we have the courage to voice our questions openly and honestly, then faith is enabled to break new ground as God leads us to a deeper understanding and greater maturity in Christ.

Lord, I believe, help my unbelief.　　Mark 9:24

Thomas said, 'Unless I see the marks of the nails in his hands, and put my finger in the mark of the nails and my hand in his side, I will not believe.'　　John 20:25b

Lord, I'm not sure any more –
　　not like I used to be.
There was a time when it was all so clear,
　　everything black and white.
But now?

I just don't know.
And I'm lost and frightened.
It's not that I don't believe any more –
    simply that the edges have become blurred,
    the picture fuzzy, no matter how I try to focus it.
And I can't say why – that's what really frightens me.
There's no one moment I can put my finger on
    and say that's where it all started,
    where the rot set in,
    where the damage was done.
It's rather that, slowly,
    like it or not,
    my view on life has changed –
    few things as certain as I once thought,
    few truths as uncomplicated as I once imagined.
What I see one way, those around me see another.
What's right in one place is wrong in the next.
What seemed obvious yesterday is a mystery today.
Why, Lord?
What's happening to me?
What's gone wrong?
I'd like it to be different,
    to be like it always was before,
    and I feel as if I'm failing you because it isn't –
    letting the side down almost,
    though that's the last thing I want to do.
Yet what option is there?
I could pretend,
    put on a show,
    go through the motions.
And yes, I might fool others,

maybe even myself.
But never you, Lord,
    that's the trouble –
    never you.

My child,
    stop torturing yourself,
    stop apologising!
I'm glad you're not sure,
    for there are few people I like less
    than those convinced of their own rightness.
Oh, I know it's not easy, living with doubt.
I know you'd love to have everything crystal clear,
    mapped out to the last detail.
But do you honestly think that would be faith?
Let me tell you this –
    if you think you know it all, you don't,
    if you imagine you've understood, you haven't,
    if you believe you've got it right,
    you've almost certainly got it wrong.
Or do you really imagine you're like me –
    your thoughts, my thoughts,
    your ways, my ways?
No, don't be ashamed of doubt,
    for it's not answers I'm looking for;
    it's a willingness to ask the questions –
    to keep on looking,
    keep on striving,
    keep on accepting there's another step
    still to be taken,

just when you thought the end was in sight.
It may be hard to live with – I'm well aware of that –
    but, believe me, it's not doubt that will destroy you,
    despite what some people may say –
    it's a faith that will not question.

For now we see in a mirror, dimly, but then we will see face to face. Now I know only in part; then I will know fully, even as I have been fully known.   1 Corinthians 13:12

I want to know Christ and the power of his resurrection and the sharing of his sufferings by becoming like him in his death, if somehow I may attain the resurrection from the dead. Not that I have already obtained this or have already reached the goal; but I press on to make it my own, because Christ Jesus has made me his own. Beloved, I do not consider that I have made it my own; but this one thing I do: forgetting what lies behind and straining forward to what lies ahead, I press on toward the goal for the prize of the heavenly call of God in Christ Jesus. Let those of us then who are mature be of the same mind; and if you think differently about anything, this too God will reveal to you. Only let us hold fast to what we have attained.   Philippians 3:10-16

Then he said to Thomas, 'Put your finger here and see my hands. Reach out your hand and put it in my side. Do not doubt but believe.' Thomas answered him, 'My Lord and my God!'
John 20:27-28

8

Me, prejudiced?

We live in an age when, quite rightly, vigorous attempts are made to overcome prejudice in society. Occasionally, we may feel this concern has been taken too far, political correctness bordering on the ridiculous, but this is a small price to pay for ensuring that people are not victimised or discriminated against because of their colour, age, sex, race, religion, social status or for any other reason. Yet a recognition of the inherent worth in everyone does not mean that we are all the same. On the contrary, no two people are ever identical. We each have something distinctive about ourselves, something to contribute to others and to receive from them in turn. It is in respecting and learning from the real differences between us and our fellow human beings, that we truly recognise both the worth in ourselves and in them.

If a person with gold rings and in fine clothes comes into your assembly, and if a poor person in dirty clothes also comes in, and if you take notice of the one wearing the fine clothes and say, 'Have a seat here, please', while to the one who is poor you say, 'Stand there', or, 'Sit at my feet', have you not made distinctions among yourselves, and become judges with evil thoughts? You do well if you really fulfil the royal law according to the scripture, 'You shall love your neighbour as yourself.' But if you show partiality, you commit sin and are convicted by the law as transgressors.

James 2:2-4, 8-9

The next day Jesus decided to go to Galilee. He found Philip and said to him, 'Follow me.' Now Philip was from Bethsaida, the city of Andrew and Peter. Philip found Nathanael and said to him, 'We have found him about whom Moses in the law and also the prophets wrote, Jesus son of Joseph from Nazareth.' Nathanael said to him, 'Can anything good come out of Nazareth?'

John 1:43-46

Me, prejudiced?
You must be joking!
I'm as open as the next person,
    more if anything.
The sort who takes folk as I find them,
    each to their own,
    live and let live.
All right, so maybe I do make the occasional slip-up,
    the inadvertent sexist comment;
    and perhaps I do sometimes jump to conclusions,
    swayed too much by appearances;
    but I don't mean it, you know that, Lord –
    the last thing I'd ever do is judge by the label.

Yet we have to be sensible,
    matter of fact about these things –
    it's one thing to accept,
    another to get involved;
    important to respect people,
    something else to rub shoulders with them.
After all, we're different, aren't we? –
    different backgrounds,
    different values,
    different customs,
    different everything.
So come on, Lord,
    you don't really expect me to mix
    with all and sundry,
    irrespective of creed or colour, do you –
    not seriously?
I'm not prejudiced –
    I'm really not –
    but they've got their lives and I've got mine,
    and quite frankly I'd rather keep it that way.

My child,
    I *am* serious, make no mistake,
    for there is more heartache caused
    by the barrier of prejudice
    than anything else I know of.
And though you think you're open,
    and want to be too,
    you *are* prejudiced,
    more than you'd imagine possible,

for deep within you,
built into the very fabric of your being,
are a multitude of preconceptions
which shape your view of the world.
You don't do it on purpose,
but every time you meet someone
you judge them –
by the way they dress,
the way they talk,
the way they think,
the way they live;
by the work they do,
and the people they mix with;
by the beliefs they hold,
and the goals they strive for.
In these and so much more your prejudice still lurks,
unrecognised,
unbeknown to you,
yet colouring your attitudes,
and fragmenting my world.
Of course people are different,
they're meant to be;
I made you that way on purpose –
to help you learn,
to stretch your minds,
and to enlarge your spirits.
And I tell you this, my child,
when you close your lives to those around you,
you close them also to me.

There is no longer Jew or Greek, there is no longer slave or free, there is no longer male and female; for all of you are one in Christ Jesus.

Galatians 3:28

As in one body we have many members, and not all the members have the same function, so we, who are many, are one body in Christ, and individually we are members one of another. We have gifts that differ according to the grace given to us. Romans 12:4-8

____9____
Another day

What would you say is the greatest social problem of our time? Homelessness? Poverty? Unemployment? Certainly there can be no denying the pain each of these causes, but let me suggest another problem, equally widespread and involving immeasurable pain. I speak of loneliness. We live in a world today where people are crying out for companionship, and I don't just mean the elderly or housebound, though for these the problem may be most acute. It is true of people from all walks of life and all ages, condemned to increasing isolation in an ever more fragmented society. For some this means the agony of scarcely meeting another human being from week to week; for others the equal, if not more intense, pain of feeling utterly alone, even when part of a crowd.

Do your best to come to me soon, for Demas, in love with this present world, has deserted me and gone to Thessalonica; Crescens has gone to Galatia, Titus to Dalmatia. Only Luke is with me. 2 Timothy 4:9-11a

Even when we came into Macedonia, our bodies had no rest, but we were afflicted in

every way – disputes without and fears within.
But God, who consoles the downcast, consoled
us by the arrival of Titus, and not only by his
coming, but also by the consolation with which
he was consoled about you, as he told us of
your longing, your mourning, your zeal for me,
so that I rejoiced still more.   2 Corinthians 7:5-7

Another day, Lord,
    another morning full of promise
    and opportunity –
    or so they tell me.
Only it isn't,
    not for me –
    it's another day just like yesterday
    and the day before,
    nothing different,
    nothing to look forward to,
    just me,
    alone,
    again.
I'll sit in the same old chair,
    stare at the same old wall,
    think the same old thoughts.
I'll watch the television programme
    I've no wish to watch,
    read the book I've no desire to read,
    knit the jumper which no one will wear,
    all in an attempt to feel a part of this world –
    a little less lonely,

a little less forgotten,
a fraction more important.
But it won't work,
for what I crave is not words but company:
the touch of a human hand,
the smile of a human face,
the warmth of a human soul –
commonplace to some perhaps,
but for me priceless,
a gift beyond measure.
Another day, Lord,
and I know I ought to thank you for it,
but I don't,
for once more I know I must live it alone.

My child,
you're not alone –
never say that.
Whatever else, I am with you,
always,
to the very end of time.
There is nothing that can keep us apart,
nothing that finally can come between us,
for even when you do not see it,
when you have no inkling as to my presence,
I am there by your side,
watching over you,
reaching out,
waiting to bless.
But yes, I know you want more than that

you want flesh and blood, real as you are –
and that's why I'm asking you to stop
and think for a moment not of *your* pain
but that of *others*,
for there's a whole world out there,
feeling just as you do,
a multitude of yearning,
aching people crying out for love.
And it doesn't take much to help them –
just a friendly word,
a gentle touch,
an outstretched hand,
and life can be different,
not just for them but you.
Pick up the telephone,
offer that invitation,
make the first move,
and the result may surprise you –
not just one prayer answered but two!
It's up to you –
you can sit back feeling sorry for yourself,
waiting for someone else to make the first move,
or you can reach out,
and discover the new day I long to give you.

*Then the Lord God said, 'It is not good that
the man should be alone; I will make him a
partner.'* Genesis 2:18

48

If I ascend to heaven, you are there; if I make my bed in Sheol, you are there. If I take the wings of the morning and settle at the farthest limits of the sea, even there your hand shall lead me, and your right hand shall hold me fast.

Psalm 139:8-10

10

I meant to do something

How often have you intended to do something and failed to do it? Probably more times than you care to remember. It's easy to make a promise, either to ourselves or others, but much harder to honour it. The reasons, of course, are many. Sometimes we just forget or we're too busy. Sometimes we find we've taken on more than we bargained for, carried away in the heat of the moment or swept along on a tide of enthusiasm, only to find, in the cold light of day, that the task we've committed ourselves to appears far less attractive. If we're lucky, our failure to do what we intended may not matter much. But sometimes it has consequences far greater than we might expect, even to the point of missing opportunities which may never come our way again.

What do you think? A man had two sons; he went to the first and said, 'Son, go and work in the vineyard today.' He answered, 'I will not'; but later he changed his mind and went. The father went to the second and said the same; and he answered, 'I go, sir'; but he did not go. Which of the two did the will of his father? They said, 'The first.' Matthew 21:28-31a

I meant to do something, I really did.
The thought was there,
   the desire.
It's just that I never got round to it,
   never quite found the time
   to turn intention into reality.
It had been on my mind for ages,
   pencilled neatly into my diary
   under items pending,
   and I'd have got round to it eventually,
   honest I would,
   despite what some might say.
It was only a matter of time –
   that's what I keep telling myself;
   I was simply waiting
   for the right moment to arrive.
But it's too late now, isn't it?
The opportunity is lost,
   the damage done,
   and there's nothing I can do about it,
   no way of turning back the clock
   and having a second stab.
I had my chance –
   it was there staring me in the face –
   and I blew it,
   putting off until tomorrow
   what I should have done today.
But you won't be too hard, Lord, will you?
You understand.
Maybe I did let you down,
   maybe I was found wanting,

but you know the thought was there,
if not the action.

My child,
        haven't you learned yet, after all this time,
        that good intentions are not enough.
It's not what you plan to do that matters,
        it's what you actually do:
        whether you put your words into action,
        your thoughts into deeds –
        that's the real test.
We can all make the right noises,
        all build heaven in our heads,
        but unless you're prepared to roll your sleeves up,
        put your money where your mouth is,
        it's not worth a penny to anyone –
        just so much empty promise.
I know you meant well,
        but don't you see what your failure has done?
You've held back my kingdom,
        frustrated my purpose,
        denied my love.
Remember that the next time and learn from it –
        that's all I ask;
        for though you can't alter what's been,
        you *can* change what's still to come.
So when the moment comes again,
        don't just think about it –
        do it!

*Not everyone who says to me, 'Lord, Lord',
will enter the kingdom of heaven, but only the
one who does the will of my Father in heaven.*
Matthew 7:21

*What good is it, my brothers and sisters, if you
say you have faith but do not have works?
Can faith save you? If a brother or sister is
naked and lacks daily food, and one of you
says to them, 'Go in peace, keep warm and
eat your fill', and yet you do not supply their
bodily needs, what is the good of that? So
faith by itself, if it has no works, is dead.*
James 2:14-17

*Little children, let us love, not in word or
speech, but in truth and action.*   1 John 3:18

11

Lord, I saw a photograph today

There's a hymn I used to sing as a boy with this chorus: 'They'll know we are Christians by our love, by our love, yes they'll know we are Christians by our love.' What a beautiful picture that paints, and how special life would be were it true. But sadly most of the time it's not. Although we warm to everything Jesus said about loving others – even our enemies – and although we want to love more than anything, the simple fact is we are not very good at it. To be honest, there are some people we find it hard even to *like*, let alone *love*. Even the love we have for ourselves and those closest to us is flawed. Yet, just occasionally, we can rise to unexpected heights of devotion – a level of selfless-ness which gives us just a glimpse of how much God loves us. And it is when we truly open our hearts to that astonishing love which sacrificed everything that love can fully flow through our lives and out to those around us.

You have heard that it was said, 'You shall love your neighbour and hate your enemy.' But I say to you, Love your enemies and pray for those who persecute you.   Matthew 5:43-44

If I speak in the tongues of mortals and of angels, but do not have love, I am a noisy gong or a clanging cymbal. And if I have prophetic powers, and understand all mysteries and all knowledge, and if I have all faith, so as to remove mountains, but do not have love, I am nothing. If I give away all my possessions, and if I hand over my body, so that I may boast, but do not have love, I gain nothing.

1 Corinthians 13:1-3

This is my commandment, that you love one another as I have loved you. No one has greater love than this, to lay down one's life for one's friends.   John 15:12-13

Lord, I saw a photograph today,
   a picture of a mother
   desperately shielding her baby
   from a hail of bullets,
   sacrificing herself to protect her little one.
And there I saw love,
   total love –
   not the pale imitation we pass off in its place,
   but the real thing,
   concerned only to give,
   pouring itself out, oblivious to the cost.
I admired that, Lord,
   and I longed to share it.
No, not the pain and sacrifice, not that,

but the ability to love
with even a fraction of that selfless devotion –
for I know deep down that I don't.
I speak of love often enough –
   sign off with it in a letter,
   send it casually over the phone –
   but it's just a word,
   well-intentioned but hollow.
And even with those dearest to me,
   my friends and family,
   though I care deeply about them –
   more than they will ever know –
   my love is still imperfect,
   as much about *me* as them –
   my happiness,
   my desires,
   my wishes,
   my well-being.
I'm not good at loving, Lord,
   and that troubles me,
   for it strikes at the very heart of my faith.
Love your enemy, love your neighbour,
   love one another –
   isn't that what you tell us to do?
And it all sounds wonderful,
   a recipe for heaven.
But it's one thing to bandy
   such fine words as theory –
   I do it all the time –
   it's another to mean them,
   let alone to make them real.

My child,
    it's quite true what you say –
    love *is* difficult,
    more costly and demanding
    than most people ever imagine;
    and it's true also that your love
    is less than it ought to be,
    as much about yourself as others.
But that's not so terrible,
    for I tell you this:
    unless you learn to love yourself
    you will never love anyone else.
Besides, there is more to you
    than you give credit for.
That picture you speak of,
    the mother shielding her child –
    you're not so different, despite what you think.
You too could rise to that
    same devotion and commitment,
    that same willingness to sacrifice all.
It would take a lot, I grant you,
    and I hope you'll never be put to the test,
    but there are those you care about enough
    to die for them if necessary.
Believe me, I know,
    for I care that much about you, about everyone,
    only it cost me more still –
    the cruellest of agonies,
    the most unimaginable pain.
I came to this world in Jesus,
    sharing your human suffering,

bearing your grief and sorrow,
and out of love I watched him give everything,
nailed to the cross so that you might live.
It was dreadful,
harder than you will ever know
not to step in and call a halt –
my child far too precious to die like that.
But I held back, honouring his wishes,
as he laid down his life for all.
So, yes, loving is difficult – I understand that –
but it's not impossible, not now anyway,
for it's been given freely,
in the blood of my Son shed for you –
and when love like that flows through your veins
it must surely soon beat in your heart.

Hatred stirs up strife, but love covers over all offences. Proverbs 10:12

Love is patient; love is kind; love is not envious or boastful or arrogant or rude. It does not insist on its own way; it is not irritable or resentful; it does not rejoice in wrongdoing, but rejoices in the truth. It bears all things, believes all things, hopes all things, endures all things. Love never ends. 1 Corinthians 13:4-8a

Beloved, let us love one another, because love is from God; everyone who loves is born of God and knows God. Whoever does not love does not know God, for God is love. God's love was revealed among us in this way: God sent his only Son into the world so that we might live through him. In this is love, not that we loved God but that he loved us and sent his Son to be the atoning sacrifice for our sins. Beloved, since God loved us so much, we also ought to love one another. No one has ever seen God; if we love one another, God lives in us, and his love is perfected in us.

1 John 4:7-12

12

I could kick myself

Even the most thick-skinned of us feel embarrassed sometimes. It's a part of life and nine times out of ten we'd probably accept the cause as of our own making. But I expect we've also all had times when, quite inadvertently, we've put our foot in it, ruffling feathers, even causing offence when that was the last thing we intended. It may be, of course, that we genuinely had no way of knowing, but we do well at such times to ask ourselves whether we were really listening, or whether our minds were too much on ourselves and too little on those we were talking to.

If there is any encouragement in Christ, any consolation from love, any sharing in the Spirit, any compassion and sympathy, make my joy complete: be of the same mind, having the same love, being in full accord and of one mind. Do nothing from selfish ambition or conceit, but in humility regard others as better than yourselves. Let each of you look not to your own interests, but to the interests of others.

Philippians 2:1-4

I could kick myself, I really could.
To think I could have been so thoughtless,
    so unfeeling,
    so insensitive.
I didn't mean any harm, Lord, you know that –
    quite the opposite –
    my only desire to show friendship,
    to let her know I cared.
But I opened my mouth too quickly,
    without stopping to check my facts,
    too full of what I could offer
    to listen to what she was saying.
And the result?
    I jumped in with both feet –
    and she ended up in tears,
    more upset than before I spoke.
Oh, she was very nice about it –
    told me it wasn't my fault,
    that I couldn't have known –
    and it's true to a point,
    but the signs were there,
    the alarm bells ringing,
    if only I'd had eyes to see and ears to hear.
Lord, I feel such a fool,
    such an idiot.
I could kick myself,
    I really could.

My child, what's all this about *you*?
Have you still not got it after all you've been through?
Of course it hurts, the memory of that mistake –
    it's meant to.
Your ego's been bruised,
    your pride dented –
    I'd be disappointed in you if it wasn't.
But you'll get over it soon enough,
    another lesson put down to experience,
    and before long you'll look back
    with a wry grin and embarrassed chuckle.
What of her, though – that's the question?
You said it yourself –
    there should have been less of you
    and more of her,
    and if that was true then it's all the more now.
She's the one you ought to be worried about –
    how she's feeling and how she'll still feel
    when for you this is all a distant memory.
So don't just sit there,
    licking your wounds,
    feeling sorry for yourself.
Don't ask me for a pat on the back,
    and a reassuring word of absolution.
Get back where you're needed,
    reach out to those who are hurting,
    try again to show you care,
    only this time stop and ask yourself
    who you're really there for –
    is it you,
    or them?

You must understand this, my beloved: let everyone be quick to listen, slow to speak.

James 1:19

Bear one another's burdens, and in this way you will fulfil the law of Christ. Galatians 6:2

13

What came over me, Lord?

There can be few of us who haven't at some time lost our temper. For those cursed with a short fuse it can be a common occurrence, whilst for those of a more phlegmatic disposition it may be something of a rarity; but all of us have our threshold where something snaps inside and we fly into a rage. There is, of course, a place for anger, as Jesus on more than one occasion shows us in the Gospels. Confronted with evil and injustice, with actions or attitudes which prevent people from living life to the full, it is not only natural but necessary. But, more often than not, anger is sparked by very different motives – wounded pride, frustration, intolerance, an unwillingness to face the truth, or simply misunderstanding. It doesn't take much to send the blood rushing to our heads, but it can take a great deal to put right the consequences of one moment's madness.

The Lord had regard for Abel and his offering, but for Cain and his offering he had no regard. So Cain was very angry, and his countenance fell. The Lord said to Cain, 'Why are you angry, and why has your countenance fallen? If you do well, will you not be accepted? And if you do not do well, sin is lurking at the door; its desire is for you, but you must master it.' Cain said to his brother Abel, 'Let us go out to the field.' And when they were in the field, Cain rose up against his brother Abel, and killed him.   Genesis 4:4b-8

Those who are hot-tempered stir up strife, but those who are slow to anger calm contention.
                                        Proverbs 15:18

Do not be quick to anger, for anger lodges in the bosom of fools.   Ecclesiastes 7:9

What came over me, Lord?
What on earth possessed me?
To think I could be so petty,
   so quick to lose my temper –
   and all over something so trivial.
I can't believe it now, looking back –
   it's as though it were some dreadful nightmare,
   some awful illusion.
But it wasn't – that's what frightens me –
   it was all too real.
And I'm to blame, nobody else –
   I lost control,
   carried away in the heat of the moment,
   red mist rising before me,
   and, before I knew it, the words were out
   and the damage was done.

I didn't mean it – you know that, Lord –
    the last thing I'd ever want is to hurt anyone,
    but that's not good enough, is it? –
    for I can still see the pain in my friend's eyes,
    the look of anguish as the shaft went home.
There's no excuse –
    whether I was right or wrong is beside the point;
    I should have stopped to think,
    taken a deep breath and counted to ten,
    but I didn't –
    I just flew off the handle,
    and now someone, somewhere,
    is left to pick up the pieces.
Forgive me, Lord, for I'm so ashamed.
Forgive me.

My child,
    is it me you should be coming to for forgiveness?
I'll give it to you gladly, just as I always do –
    and, yes, I'm glad you've come,
    glad your sorry.
But it's not me you hurt, is it?
I can forgive you all you like,
    but it's not going to take away
    that look you speak of,
    those wounded, troubled eyes.
They'll still be there, haunting you day and night,
    following you wherever you run,
    wherever you hide,
    until you've made your peace.

There's only one way to change that,
    and again it rests with you,
    no one else.
You caused the problem,
    you alone can cure it,
It may be unpleasant,
    it may be costly,
    and it may be thrown back in your face,
    but the only one who can pick up the pieces
    and put them together again is you.
So go now,
    swallow your pride,
    admit you were wrong,
    say you're sorry and ask for forgiveness.
And maybe,
    just maybe,
    if you're lucky enough to be given another chance,
    next time you are put to the test
    you will think first,
    and act later.

Whoever is slow to anger has great understanding, but one who has a hasty temper exalts folly.   Proverbs 14:29

A fool gives full vent to anger, but the wise quietly holds it back.   Proverbs 29:11

Be angry but do not sin; do not let the sun go down on your anger, and do not make room for the devil.   Ephesians 4:26-27

You must understand this, my beloved: let everyone be quick to listen, slow to speak, slow to anger; for your anger does not produce God's righteousness. James 1:19-20

___14___
Why, Lord?

Of all the mysteries of life and faith, none is harder to reconcile than the problem of suffering. How is it, we ask, that a supposedly loving and caring God can allow so much pain and misery to rack our world? Across the centuries greater minds than mine have wrestled with this conundrum yet failed to come up with a complete answer, and no doubt many more will do the same in years to come. There are no easy words or comfortable solutions – only the conviction of faith that God is there within our sorrow, sharing the pain, experiencing the grief, reaching out to the broken, suffering with those who suffer. For reasons we cannot fathom, such things are an integral part of creation which even God himself is caught up in, until that day when there will be no more pain, no more tears, and he will be all in all.

Why, O Lord, do you stand far off? Why do you hide yourself in times of trouble?

Psalm 10:1

My God, my God, why have you forsaken me? Why are you so far from helping me, from the words of my groaning? O my God, I

*cry by day, but you do not answer; and by
night, but find no rest.*   Psalm 22:1-2

*Why did I not die at birth, come forth from
the womb and expire? Now I would be lying
down and quiet; I would be asleep; then I
would be at rest. Why is light given to one in
misery, and life to the bitter in soul, who long
for death, but it does not come? Why is light
given to the one who cannot see the way,
whom God has fenced in? For my sighing
comes like my bread, and my groanings are
poured out like water. Truly the thing that I
fear comes upon me, and what I dread befalls
me. I am not at ease, nor am I quiet; I have
no rest; but trouble comes.*

Job 3:11, 13, 20-21a, 23-26

Why, Lord?
I know I shouldn't ask that,
    but I just can't help it,
    for I'm troubled,
    unable to make sense of this faith of mine,
    unable to make sense of anything.
It doesn't worry me usually,
    for I can avoid the issues,
    thankful that they don't touch me,
    not yet anyway.
But today I've been surrounded by suffering,
    by the sheer weight of human need,

and it's got to me in a way it rarely has before.
I visited the hospital,
    and saw my friend there in the cancer ward,
    curled up in bed,
    eyes sunken,
    teeth gritted against the pain –
    the operation over, but the prognosis grim.
I left him, blinking back the tears,
    but there were others,
    so many others,
    looking across the ward at me
    with pain, fear and sorrow in their eyes.
I went on to the nursing home to see another friend,
    once so vibrant, so full of life,
    but now her mind gone, her body withered –
    a mocking shadow of her former self,
    waiting for the merciful release of death.
I was glad to leave, Lord,
    glad to get out into the fresh air away from it all;
    but then an ambulance raced past, sirens blaring,
    a drunken vagrant stumbled by the roadside,
    and across the street
    a young boy grimaced in a wheelchair,
    limbs twisted, mouth dribbling.
It was everywhere,
    human suffering crying out in defiant protest –
    on the front of the newspaper,
    the car radio, the television news –
    another murder, another rape,
    another war, another tragedy;
    and suddenly, Lord,

as I stared starkly into the darkness,
I could hold it back no longer –
the inevitable question:
why?

My child,
   don't be ashamed of asking,
   for I don't blame you,
   not in the slightest.
On the contrary,
   my only surprise is that it took you so long,
   for it's not as it should be, this world I've made,
   not as I want it,
   nor as I planned it.
I look upon it day after day,
   the pain and sorrow,
   the hatred and cruelty,
   and it breaks my heart to see the beauty I intended
   so cruelly disfigured,
   laughter turning to despair,
   joy into tragedy.
That's why I came through my Son,
   sharing your humanity and bearing your sorrow –
   to ensure that one day it will be different,
   the time coming
   when there will be no more suffering,
   tears or darkness.
It will come, believe me,
   but the time must be right,
   and, until then, as well as joy

there must be sorrow,
    as well as pleasure, pain,
    as well as life, death,
    each a part of a fallen, broken world.
Yet seen or unseen,
    recognised or unrecognised,
    I am there with you,
    not watching from the sidelines, casually aloof,
    nor safely at a distance,
    untouched and unmoved,
    but sharing in your hurt,
    aching with those who ache,
    groaning with those who groan,
    weeping with those who weep.
I cannot stop your pain,
    but I can help bear it,
    and though you'll still have doubts
    and still ask why,
    I can only say:
    hold on to me,
    as I keep hold of you.

Rise up, O Lord; O God, lift up your hand; do not forget the oppressed. You do see! Indeed, you note trouble and grief, that you may take it into your hands; the helpless commit themselves to you.   Psalm 10:12, 14

I am utterly bowed down and prostrate; all day long I go around mourning. For my loins are filled with burning, and there is no sound-ness in my flesh. I am utterly spent and crushed; I groan because of the tumult of my heart. O Lord, all my longing is known to you; my sighing is not hidden from you. My heart throbs, my strength fails me; as for the light of my eyes – it also has gone from me. My friends and companions stand aloof from my affliction, and my neighbours stand afar off. But it is for you, O Lord, that I wait; it is you, O Lord my God, who will answer. Do not forsake me, O Lord; O my God, do not be far from me; make haste to help me, O Lord, my salvation.   Psalm 38:6-11, 15, 21-22

15

I'll never forget it

There are moments for us all which will live on in our memory for as long as we live. For me such a time came many years ago during my very first holiday on the Isle of Wight. I was walking with my parents and brothers and sisters over the downs on the west of the island, when, reaching the crest of a hill, we were unexpectedly confronted by the most glorious of sights. There ahead of us, framed by the vivid purple of the heather, the whiteness of the cliffs, the dazzling blue of sea and sky, and the soft green of the grass, was the celebrated Needles Lighthouse, a picture postcard scene if ever there was one. To me it was like a dream, and there have been many times since when I have stood in my imagination at that same spot gazing out with the same sense of awe and wonder. No doubt each of us will be able to recall similar experiences; moments when we simply stood and stared, rejoicing in the beauty of creation, giving thanks to God for the sheer loveliness of this world. We need to hold on to such memories, and take them back with us into the everyday routine of life, conscious that God is there as much as anywhere.

Sing to the Lord with thanksgiving; make melody to our God on the lyre. He covers the heavens with clouds, prepares rain for the earth, makes grass grow on the hills. He gives animals their food, and to the young ravens when they cry. He sends out his command to the earth; his word runs swiftly. He gives snow like wool; he scatters frost like ashes. He hurls down hail like crumbs – who can stand before his cold? He sends out his word, and melts them; he makes his wind blow, and the waters flow. Psalm 147:7-9, 15-18

Praise the Lord! Praise the Lord from the heavens; praise him in the heights! Praise him, sun and moon; praise him, all you shining stars! Let them praise the name of the Lord, for he commanded and they were created. Mountains and all hills, fruit trees and all cedars! Wild animals and all cattle, creeping things and flying birds! Let them praise the name of the Lord, for his name alone is exalted; his glory is above earth and heaven.

Psalm 148:1, 3, 5, 9-10, 13

I'll never forget it, Lord,
    that moment as I stood on that hilltop
    and took in the sight before me –
    the sun golden on the horizon,
    the sea stretching out into the distance,

blue as topaz,
the cliffs white as snow,
and the seagulls soaring overhead
in lofty splendour.
It was magnificent,
a taste of paradise,
the world as I'd never seen it before,
full of beauty and wonder.
I heard cows lowing and sheep calling their young,
birds singing in the distance
and bees droning among the heather,
the laughter of the waves
and the playful whispering of grass
stirred by the breeze,
each joining to create a jubilant chorus,
an outpouring of celebration,
a hymn of praise.
And my heart joined in the dance,
leaping with delight,
skipping with pleasure,
crying out in adoration.
For here was freedom and inexpressible loveliness,
life as it ought to be,
creation in all its glory.
It was wonderful, Lord,
a glimpse of your majesty,
a revelation of your handiwork,
a sign of your love –
and in that moment, as never before,
I gave you my worship.

My child,
> this may come as a surprise,
> but that moment was precious to me
> as well as you,
> for the wonder in your eyes
> and the joy in your face
> was a prayer greater than all words,
> an expression of gratitude I shall always treasure.

So thank you for your worship,
> and thank you for taking time to stop and stare,
> to glimpse my presence in the beauty of creation,
> to reflect on my handiwork
> and know me by your side.

Don't lose that sense of awe,
> for it is a gateway to heaven,
> a foretaste of my eternal kingdom.

Yet remember also there is more to discover –
> that if you found me once
> in a moment of quietness,
> you must find me always
> in every place and every moment.

Make time to withdraw, of course,
> but then return,
> back to the daily round of life.

Make time to pause,
> but then resume,
> picking up where you left off.

Make time to reflect,
> but then to act,
> seeing my presence in the place
> where I have placed you,

for when you have learned that, my child,
we shall dance together for all eternity.

*O Lord, our Sovereign, how majestic is your
name in all the earth!* Psalm 8:1

*The heavens are declaring the glory of God;
and the firmament proclaims his handiwork.
Day to day pours forth speech, and night to
night declares knowledge. There is no speech,
nor are there words; their voice is not heard;
yet their voice goes out through all the earth,
and their words to the end of the world.*
Psalm 19:1-4

*The earth is the Lord's and all that is in it, the
world, and those who live in it; for he has
founded it on the seas, and established it on
the rivers.* Psalm 24:1-2

16

God, I'm scared!

Of all the destructive forces at work within us, few, I believe, are more powerful than fear. I don't mean the fear we all feel sometimes when confronted by danger, but rather that dull nagging anxiety which can creep into our lives almost unnoticed and then slowly take over. Such fear saps us of energy, drains us of self-confidence, and robs us of enthusiasm. At its most extreme it can result in inexplicable feelings of panic, even complete breakdown. It is hardly surprising, then, that our natural instinct is to run away from our fears, and to stifle as best we can any such feeling within us. Yet this is a recipe for disaster. The only way to conquer fear is to confront it, in the knowledge that, with God on our side, nothing can finally harm us.

Truly the thing that I fear comes upon me, and what I dread befalls me. I am not at ease, nor am I quiet; I have no rest; but trouble comes.

Job 3:25-26

God, I'm scared!
Don't tell anyone I told you,
    for there's no knowing what they'll think,
    but I'm petrified,
    more frightened than I can ever say,
    and the terrible thing is I don't know why.
You think that sounds stupid?
Well, yes, it probably is,
    but you see there's no single factor
    I can put my finger on,
    no simple explanation for this fear I'm feeling.
It's more a combination of everything –
    all the little anxieties,
    the nagging doubts,
    the constant demands –
    all coming together to overwhelm me.
I can feel it now, beavering away within,
    gnawing into my very soul,
    and I'm powerless to stop it –
    the harder I try, the more tenaciously it clings,
    the more I resist,
    the more I wake up and find it there to greet me.
I walk down the street, and it's there by my side.
I meet a stranger, even a friend,
    and it leers out at me.
I look longingly to the future but it's there too,
    waiting for me.
Lord, is there nowhere I can escape,
    nowhere I can be free?

My child,
    don't be afraid,
    I'm here –
    no need to panic.
Let's look at these fears of yours,
    slowly and sensibly.
You tell me you're not afraid of one thing in particular,
    and you're right,
    for if you were
    you'd have come to terms with it by now,
    sorted it out once and for all.
No, it's a deeper problem you're suffering from –
    the fear of fear itself,
    and that's something much harder to deal with,
    a dilemma only you finally can resolve.
You need to stop running,
    stop looking over your shoulder,
    and face your fear head on.
You need to stop brooding,
    stop struggling,
    and let it do its worst.
When you do that you'll realise
    this monster of your imagination
    is just an empty phantom,
    powerless to touch you,
    still less to hurt.
It won't be easy at first,
    for you must change the habit of a lifetime,
    but trust me,
    remember I am with you,
    pay heed to my words,

and, before you know it,
your fears will be fleeing from you,
rather than you from them.

*Even though I walk through the darkest valley,
I fear no evil; for you are with me; your rod
and your staff they comfort me.*   Psalm 23:4

*Though an army encamp against me, my heart
shall not fear; though war rise up against me,
yet will I be confident.*   Psalm 27:3

*With the Lord on my side I do not fear. What
can mortals do to me?*   Psalm 118:6

*Do not be afraid of sudden panic, or of the
storm that strikes the wicked; for the Lord will
be your confidence and will keep your foot
from being caught.*   Proverbs 3:25-26

17

God, I'm busy

We live today, so we are told, in stressful times. Despite having labour-saving gadgets such as our grandparents could only have dreamt of, and corresponding leisure time to enjoy into the bargain, we are part of an increasingly pressurised world. Exhaustion and burn-out are the afflictions of our age, as we attempt to cram yet more activity into our already overcrowded lives. The rewards may be great, but so also may the cost. It is worth sometimes just pausing for breath and asking ourselves, 'Is it all worth it?'

Martha was distracted by her many tasks; so she came to him and asked, 'Lord, do you not care that my sister has left me to do all the work by myself? Tell her then to help me.' But the Lord answered her, 'Martha, Martha, you are worried and distracted by many things; there is need of only one thing. Mary has chosen the better part, which will not be taken away from her.' Luke 10:40-42

Why do you spend your money for that which is not bread, and your labour for that which does not satisfy? Isaiah 55:2

*What do mortals get from all the toil and strain
with which they toil under the sun? For all their
days are full of pain, and their work is a vexa-
tion; even at night their minds do not rest. This
also is vanity.*   Ecclesiastes 2:22-23

God, I'm busy,
    rushed off my feet,
    running around like a headless chicken
    with scarcely a moment to breathe.
I hardly know what I'm doing one day to the next,
    always something else waiting,
    someone else demanding my time –
    another job,
    another need,
    another cry for help.
Lord, I'm exhausted,
    just about fit to drop,
    for I've given everything,
    the last drop of blood.
Yet I can't afford to stop,
    not yet anyway,
    for if I do, who will pick up the pieces,
    who will ensure the job gets done?
I've done my best – no one can argue with that –
    but there's so much still to do
    and so little time to do it.
Lord, give me strength,
    give me a break,
    give me *something*!

My child,
    you are busy,
    your energy astonishing –
    I honestly don't know how you do it!
But be careful, please,
    for even you need to stop some time.
You can't take on everything, and you mustn't try,
    however strong the urge may be.
I know it's hard to leave a job undone,
    a task unfinished,
    but occasionally you need to,
    or you'll pay the price –
    believe me, I've seen it all too often.
So step back a little,
    and think about what you're doing
    and why you're doing it?
Is it really so urgent?
Won't it wait till tomorrow?
Does it have to be you?
You see, sometimes we can be so busy
    we lose sight of what really matters.
There's a time for busyness, don't get me wrong,
    for doing instead of simply talking,
    but there's a time also for being still
    and reflecting on what really counts.
So stop a minute and pause for breath,
    for perhaps then,
    and only then,
    you may find the rest that you crave.

Be still, and know that I am God.   Psalm 46:10a

For thus said the Lord God, the Holy One of Israel: In returning and rest you shall be saved; in quietness and in trust shall be your strength.
Isaiah 30:15

Come to me, all you that are weary and are carrying heavy burdens, and I will give you rest. Take my yoke upon you, and learn from me; for I am gentle and humble in heart, and you will find rest for your souls. For my yoke is easy, and my burden is light.
Matthew 11:28-30

———— 18 ————
Lord, I had no idea

How well do you know those you mix with – your family or friends, your colleagues at work or fellow church members? You may think you know them well, but do you? There have been many times when, talking to a friend of long standing, I have unexpectedly learned something about them which gives a whole new insight into their character and history. Actions which before made no sense suddenly fit into place; words which left me puzzled find a simple explanation; and the experience can be profoundly humbling, bringing home all too sharply how easily and often we make judgements about people based on the flimsiest of facts about them. Perhaps more disturbing still is the realisation that others form conclusions about us in much the same way. No wonder Jesus told his followers to judge not, lest they be judged.

Do not speak evil against one another, brothers and sisters. There is one lawgiver and judge who is able to save and to destroy. So who, then, are you to judge your neighbour?

James 4:11a, 12

Do not judge by appearances, but judge with right judgement. John 7:24

Lord, I had no idea – do you realise that?
Despite all the years of knowing him,
    all the time we'd spent together,
    I had no idea what he'd been through
    or what made him tick.
I thought I had –
    I actually imagined I understood him,
    but today I stopped and listened,
    giving him the confidence to open up,
    and it changed everything.
Just one little detail, that's all it took,
    one telling revelation,
    and suddenly I saw this man I thought I knew
    in a changed light,
    from an altogether different perspective,
    glimpsing a character infinitely more complex
    than I'd ever dreamt.
It made sense of everything:
    the unexplained words,
    the puzzling deeds –
    each coming together to complete the jigsaw,
    and with it all in place,
    the picture complete,
    I realised the image I had of him
    could hardly have been more wrong.
I'm ashamed, Lord,
    for I dared to sit in judgement
    although I had no right,
    I presumed to know so much
    when I understood so little;
    and the result said more about me than anyone.

My child,
    you have been foolish,
    and you should have known better,
    but I'm not sure you see why,
    despite what you say.
It's true you had no idea
    what your friend had been through,
    and it's just possible,
    had there been less of you and more of him,
    less jumping to conclusions
    and more time to listen,
    you'd have understood sooner
    and acted differently.
But you can't be sure of that,
    for in everyone you meet
    there is always more to discover,
    even those you've known a lifetime,
    and no matter how hard you try
    you will never know it all,
    nor even skim the surface.
You may hear their words,
    but you can't read their minds.
You may see their actions,
    but never their hearts.
Yet this is what counts,
    not the outside but the inside,
    where I alone can see.
And that's where you made your mistake, my child,
    where you got things so wrong –
    not in judging unfairly,
    but in presuming to judge at all.

Do not judge, so that you may not be judged. For with the judgement you make you will be judged, and the measure you give will be the measure you get. Why do you see the speck in your neighbour's eye, but do not notice the log in your own eye? Or how can you say to your neighbour, 'Let me take the speck out of your eye', while the log is in your own eye? You hypocrite, first take the log out of your own eye, and then you will see clearly to take the speck out of your neighbour's eye.

Matthew 7:1-5

Why do you pass judgement on your brother or sister? Or you, why do you despise your brother or sister? For we will all stand before the judgement seat of God. For it is written, 'As I live, says the Lord, every knee shall bow to me, and every tongue shall give praise to God.' So then, each of us will be accountable to God. Let us therefore no longer pass judgement on one another, but resolve instead never to put a stumbling block or hindrance in the way of another. Romans 14:10-13

___19___

I'm worried

It's hard sometimes not to worry. We may know it achieves little, but when we or our loved ones are facing some kind of threat to our well-being, it's difficult to be rational about things. And let's face it, we wouldn't be human if every problem, no matter how great, just rolled off us like water off a duck's back. Yet, left unchecked, worry can take over our whole life, reducing us to a shadow of the person we are meant to be.

Anxiety weighs down the human heart, but a good word cheers it up. Proverbs 12:25

Cast all your anxiety on him, because he cares for you. 1 Peter 5:7

Come to me, all you that are weary and are carrying heavy burdens, and I will give you rest. Take my yoke upon you, and learn from me; for I am gentle and humble in heart, and you will find rest for your souls. For my yoke is easy, and my burden is light. Matthew 11:28-30

I'm worried, Lord,
    more than I've ever been in my life.
I know I shouldn't be –
    there are enough people telling me that –
    but I just can't help it,
    the more I struggle to stay calm,
    the more worried I become.
It just adds another anxiety to all the rest,
    and there are enough of those already,
    aren't there? –
    health,
    money,
    work,
    family –
    never allowing a moment's peace.
Time and again, despite my efforts,
    I catch myself brooding,
    haunted by a multitude of questions
    about the future –
    and all the time the spectre grows
    of life spinning crazily out of control,
    taking all I value with it.
It's easy to say, 'Don't worry',
    that everything will be all right,
    but what if it isn't,
    what if my fears come true?
What then, Lord?

My child,
  you know what I'm going to say, don't you?
That's right – don't worry!
But before you jump down my throat,
  stop and hear me out.
I'm not pretending everything will come good,
  for I know it doesn't sometimes –
  all too rarely for my liking.
And I'm not saying your fears are unfounded,
  for sadly some of them probably aren't.
But what I am telling you is this:
  the only thing worry will change is *you* –
  for the worse.
It won't make you feel any better,
  that somehow you have everything sorted.
It won't stop your fears coming true,
  still less help you face them if they do.
On the contrary, it will suck you dry,
  sap you of energy,
  rob you of the very strength you will need
  should crisis come.
That's one reason I tell you not to worry –
  because I see what it does to you
  and know it achieves nothing.
But there's another reason, more important still,
  for the main thing is I love you,
  and understand your needs,
  and care about your welfare
  more than you would ever imagine.
No, I can't promise you a bed of roses –
  that's not the way I work –

but I do guarantee this:
whatever you face,
however many nightmares come true,
I'll be there with you always,
come what may,
to see you through.

*I tell you, do not worry about your life, what
you will eat or what you will drink, or about
your body, what you will wear. Is not life more
than food, and the body more than clothing?
Look at the birds of the air; they neither sow
nor reap nor gather into barns, and yet your
heavenly Father feeds them. Are you not of
more value than they? And can any of you by
worrying add a single hour to your span of life?
And why do you worry about clothing? Consider
the lilies of the field, how they grow; they neither
toil nor spin, yet I tell you, even Solomon in
all his glory was not clothed like one of these.
But if God so clothes the grass of the field,
which is alive today and tomorrow is thrown
into the oven, will he not much more clothe
you – you of little faith? Therefore do not worry,
saying, 'What will we eat?' or 'What will we
drink?' or 'What will we wear?' For it is the
Gentiles who strive for all these things; and
indeed your heavenly Father knows that you
need all these things. But strive first for the
kingdom of God and his righteousness, and*

all these things will be given to you as well. So do not worry about tomorrow, for tomorrow will bring worries of its own. Today's trouble is enough for today. Matthew 6:25-34

Peace I leave with you; my peace I give to you. I do not give to you as the world gives. Do not let your hearts be troubled, and do not let them be afraid. John 14:27

20

Lord, teach me to say sorry

There is one word which, if we could learn to say it more often, has the power to change the world we live in. But it is probably one of the hardest words to say. I'm referring, of course, to that little word 'sorry' – a word which should be so simple, yet which sticks in the throat as few others do. We can mean to say it, we can look for the opportunity, but when the moment of truth comes, so often we are unable to spit it out. The reason I suppose is our reluctance to lose face, our unwillingness publicly to admit our fallibility. Yet although some might see saying sorry as a sign of weakness, it actually requires great humility and immense courage. If only more of us were brave enough to give it a go.

I confess my iniquity; I am sorry for my sin.
Psalm 38:18

I will get up and go to my father, and I will say to him, 'Father, I have sinned against heaven and before you; I am no longer worthy to be called your son; treat me like one of your hired hands.' Luke 15:18-19

> *When you are offering your gift at the altar, if you remember that your brother or sister has something against you, leave your gift there before the altar and go; first be reconciled to your brother or sister, and then come and offer your gift.* Matthew 5:23-24

Lord, teach me to say sorry –
    that's my prayer today.
Simple enough, you might think,
    and it is,
    or it should be,
    yet it's a word I find so difficult.
Not with you, I've no problem there,
    nor myself either, that's the strange thing –
    I know my mistakes well enough,
    and am happy to admit them,
    to get them off my chest.
But with others it's a different story –
    I see my faults, all right, the hurt I've caused;
    I know I've acted falsely, unfairly wronged them –
    and yet, although I long to make amends,
    the word just will not come.
I mean to say it, I really do,
    and I look for the opportunity to make a move,
    yet when the moment comes,
    I back away and bite my tongue.
I'm ashamed, Lord,
    ashamed of all the needless pain so many bear,
    the broken trust and wounded hearts,

because I will not bend.
But I know it's not you I should apologise to –
    it's them.

My child,
    are you serious?
I'd like to think so, but I'm not sure you are,
    for what then are you waiting for?
You've told me the answer along with the problem,
    so why are you still standing there talking?
It's as you say,
    down to the last detail –
    your apologies are due not to me
    but those you've wronged.
You may be sorry,
    but that means nothing, not unless you show it,
    and until you do, the heartache you've caused
    will go on growing
    and the rift you've created yawn ever deeper.
It can only get harder, the longer you leave it,
    you know that, don't you? –
    the right moment you're waiting for,
    the perfect opportunity you hope to find
    always just out of reach.
So no more excuses,
    no more shirking the issue –
    it's time to grasp the nettle,
    to put this behind you once and for all,
    to make your peace and heal the wounds.
It's time to say sorry.

Blessed are the peacemakers, for they will be called children of God.   Matthew 5:9

If it is possible, so far as it depends on you, live peaceably with all.   Romans 12:18

Put things in order, agree with one another, live in peace; and the God of love and peace will be with you.   2 Corinthians 13:11

Confess your sins to one another.   James 5:16a

21

I don't want to be rich

Week after week millions of people across the country sit in front of their television sets and hope against hope that their six lucky numbers will come up in the National Lottery. Why? For a bit of fun? A playful flutter? A bit of entertainment? Hardly! It's because each one dreams of being rich, of having more money than they know what to do with, of being able to escape from the drudgery of their daily routine and live the life of their dreams. And let's be honest, which of us would sneeze at a million-pound bonanza? It's all very well to claim, after yet another blank night, that we wouldn't really want to be rich anyway, but, if the opportunity came, few of us would spurn the chance. Yet it remains true that wealth cannot guarantee happiness, and may just as easily destroy it. A cliché it may be, but the best things in life really are free. True riches can never be measured in money, and, if we but realised it, most of us have treasures beyond our imagining.

> He said to them, 'Take care! Be on your guard against all kinds of greed; for one's life does not consist in the abundance of possessions.' Then he told them a parable: 'The land of a

rich man produced abundantly. And he thought to himself, "What should I do, for I have no place to store my crops?" Then he said, "I will do this: I will pull down my barns and build larger ones, and there I will store all my grain and my goods. And I will say to my soul, 'Soul, you have ample goods laid up for many years; relax, eat, drink, be merry.'" But God said to him, "You fool! This very night your life is being demanded of you. And the things you have prepared, whose will they be?" So it is with those who store up treasures for themselves but are not rich towards God.'   Luke 12:15-21

The miser is in a hurry to get rich and does not know that loss is sure to come.

Proverbs 28:22

The lover of money will not be satisfied with money; nor the lover of wealth, with gain.

Ecclesiastes 5:10

I don't want to be rich, Lord,
   seriously –
   more trouble than it's worth, I shouldn't wonder,
   but I wouldn't mind a few extra pounds,
   enough to make me comfortable,
   to buy those little luxuries I've always wanted,
   that foreign holiday,
   that suite of furniture,
   that new car.

Am I asking too much, Lord?
I've scrimped and saved all these years,
   worked myself to the bone, day in, day out,
   and never once complained –
   well, not often anyway.
Why should I? – I've been happy by and large.
After all, money can't buy you happiness, can it?
Isn't that what they say?
But sometimes,
   just occasionally,
   I can't help looking at those around me,
   the way some of them live,
   and wondering about the justice of it all,
   why they should have so much and I so little.
Isn't it my turn, Lord –
   time for me to have my place at the party,
   my share of the cake?
I don't mean to be greedy, I really don't,
   but it would be nice just once in a lifetime
   to be able to push the boat out,
   treat myself, my friends and my family,
   without always measuring what I'd like to give
   with what I know I can afford.

My child,
   I'm sorry if you feel hard done by, truly I am,
   though I can understand it,
   for there's all too much in the world
   that's not as it should be,
   much that is less than fair.

I see the rich get richer and the poor get poorer,
    and I cry out for justice.
But my voice is rarely heard,
    drowned by the jangle of cash tills
    and rustling of wallets.
I wish everyone could be rewarded fairly,
    all of you enjoy a proper share
    of this world's resources,
    but by your own admission
    there's more to happiness than money.
You can be rich beyond words
    but utterly wretched,
    have more money than you could ever spend
    yet be empty within,
    for the things that matter, which truly satisfy,
    cannot be bought.
They are beyond price,
    beyond measuring,
    yet free to all.
So don't pin your hopes on that elusive jackpot,
    that surprise legacy,
    that lucky find.
I can't promise you wealth,
    and to be honest I wouldn't want to,
    but what I do offer,
    and what I long to give you,
    are these:
    peace,
    joy,
    love,
    hope,

life –
and if all those aren't riches,
then I don't know what is.

Better is a little with the fear of the Lord than great treasure and trouble with it. Better is a dinner of vegetables where love is than a fatted ox and hatred with it.   Proverbs 15:16-17

Better is a little with righteousness than large income with injustice.   Proverbs 16:8

Do not wear yourself out to get rich; be wise enough to desist. When your eyes light upon it, it is gone; for suddenly it takes wings to itself, flying like an eagle toward heaven.
                                                          Proverbs 23:4-5

There is great gain in godliness combined with contentment; for we brought nothing into the world, so that we can take nothing out of it; but if we have food and clothing, we will be content with these. But those who want to be rich fall into temptation and are trapped by many senseless and harmful desires that plunge people into ruin and destruction. For the love of money is the root of all kinds of evil, and in their eagerness to be rich some have wandered away from the faith and pierced themselves with many pains. As for those who in the present age are rich, command them not to be haughty, or to set their hopes on the uncertainty of riches, but rather on God who richly provides us with everything for our enjoyment. They are to do good, to be rich in good works, generous, and ready to share, thus storing up for themselves the treasure of a good foundation for the future, so that they may take hold of the life that really is life.

1 Timothy 6:6-10, 17-19

— 22 —
He smiled

Anybody who has ever spent time with a little child must surely have been touched by the experience. There is something about the very young – their honesty, their openness, their innocence, their simple trust, and their unquenchable zest for life – which has the power to move even the hardest of hearts in a way few other things can. Sadly, as time passes, much of all that is inevitably lost. We have to become worldly-wise in order to survive, and even perhaps world-weary. Our idealism is blunted on the anvil of experience, to the point sometimes of downright cynicism. Rightly or wrongly, we learn to conceal our thoughts and emotions behind a socially acceptable mask. Yet, though much which is childish is by necessity outgrown, there are certain childlike qualities we lose at our peril.

People were bringing little children to him in order that he might touch them; and the disciples spoke sternly to them. But when Jesus saw this, he was indignant and said to them, 'Let the little children come to me; do not stop them; for it is to such as these that the kingdom of God belongs. Truly I tell you, whoever does not receive the kingdom of God as a little child will never enter it.' And

*he took them up in his arms, laid his hands
on them, and blessed them.*   Mark 10:13-16

He smiled, Lord,
    the sweet innocent smile of childhood –
    and I was captivated,
    overwhelmed by the simple beauty
    of that moment.
For here was unadulterated happiness,
    a look of sheer joy,
    devoid of guile,
    untouched by the darker side of life.
I wanted to hold on to that, Lord,
    to keep the world with all its perils at bay,
    to stop the clock and preserve my child
    just as he was,
    in all his purity and trust.
But I couldn't, of course,
    and he wouldn't have wanted me to,
    for life moves on –
    new challenges,
    new horizons,
    new avenues to tread
    and experiences to explore –
    and although much must be lost in that journey,
    much also will be gained.
I knew that, Lord,
    and I resolved to respect it,
    yet I still shed a tear for the beauty of that smile,
    and the sweetness of that face.

My child,
  it *is* special, isn't it, the innocence of a little one?
A treasure beyond price,
  the most precious of gifts.
And it *is* sad that so much is lost as the years go by,
  battered and bruised by the daily round of life.
But must it *all* be lost?
I don't think so.
Tempered perhaps,
  refined through experience,
  yet not destroyed.
You still need the ability, whatever your age,
  to look through a child's eyes –
  to gaze with wonder, and hunger for knowledge,
  to laugh with abandonment,
  and dance with delight,
  to speak with candour, and act without reserve,
  to respond with love, and reach out in trust.
Lose that –
  let go of the little one inside you –
  and you lose everything,
  your very soul,
  for it is those who are like children
  who will see my face,
  those who will not only inherit
  the kingdom of heaven
  but have entered it already.

He sat down, called the twelve, and said to them, 'Whoever wants to be first must be last of all and servant of all.' Then he took a little child and put it among them; and taking it in his arms, he said to them, 'Whoever welcomes one such child in my name welcomes me, and whoever welcomes me welcomes not me but the one who sent me.' Mark 9:35-37

__ 23 __
I'm trapped

'They're painfully shy, you know.' We've probably all heard words like those used to describe somebody we know, and we understand exactly what is meant, for there are some people so reserved, so withdrawn, so tongue-tied, that it is indeed almost painful to be with them. Yet, however much *we* may suffer at such times, it is almost certainly nothing compared with the agony the individual in question is going through. If you have ever been shy, you'll know that. It is hard to overstate the sense of isolation and anguish shyness brings – at its worst, a feeling of absolute helplessness, frustration and despair. But if that is how you feel – and more of us do than you might think – don't lose heart, for at the centre of our faith is the conviction that we matter to God; that in his eyes we are *all* worth something.

Moses said to the Lord, 'O my Lord, I have never been eloquent, neither in the past nor even now that you have spoken to your servant; but I am slow of speech and slow of tongue. O my Lord, please send someone else.'

Exodus 4:10, 13

I'm trapped, Lord,
    trapped in a web of my own weaving,
    and the harder I try to break free,
    the more tangled I become.
I feel powerless,
    impotent,
    governed by forces outside my control.
Yet I shouldn't –
    it's beyond reason –
    for there's no spiteful demon
    spinning the threads that bind me;
    only me and my foolish fear of others.
It hurts, Lord,
    and what makes it harder is that no one realises.
They think I don't want to know –
    that I'm cold,
    aloof,
    distant –
    when all I want, more than anything,
    is to be like them –
    one of the crowd,
    a part of their world.
I've tried to conquer it, Lord, this shyness of mine,
    I've tried everything,
    yet the harder I struggle to break out,
    the deeper I'm sucked in.
Always it's the same old story –
    when the moment comes and I catch their eyes,
    my mind goes blank and I smile inanely,
    blushing like a child,
    stammering in confusion . . .

and then wandering off alone.
Lord, set me free from myself.

My child,
     don't despair.
I'm listening.
I've heard your cry,
     and I understand what you're saying.
But you've got things wrong,
     back to front and inside out!
I'll set you free, willingly,
     but not *from* yourself, never that.
Don't you realise *I* made you,
     as you *are*,
     with all your strengths and skills,
     foibles and foolishness.
I made you, as I made *everyone*,
     unique,
     precious,
     special.
So why do you undervalue yourself?
What are you afraid of?
I realise you don't find sharing easy,
     but neither do others, if you only knew –
     so many, like yourself,
     locked in their own private prison.
It grieves me, desperately,
     for it's not what I want for anyone.
I want you to *be* yourself,
     set free from anything which prevents that,

and you can be, if you'll only do one thing.
Forget what *others* may think –
    it's what *I* think that matters,
    and *I* believe you're important,
    with as much to offer
    and as much right to be here as the next person.
So go out and be who you are,
    openly,
    honestly,
    without apology –
    and let that be enough.

God created humankind in his image, in the image of God he created them; male and female he created them.   Genesis 1:27

What are human beings that you are mindful of them, mortals that you care for them? Yet you have made them a little lower than God, and crowned them with glory and honour.
Psalm 8:4-5

24

You're here, Lord!

Some years ago I came across the following words in a little collection of quotations: 'Life must be lived forwards, but it can only be understood backwards.' So observed the Danish theologian Soren Kierkegaard. And there's a lot of truth in that observation. So often we cannot make sense of our existence from one day to another. We look for a purpose but see only a riddle. Faith itself can struggle to hold on, faced with the apparent inactivity of God. Yet which of us, with the benefit of hindsight, haven't looked back and recognised God's hand at work in our lives when we were least aware of it?

I cry aloud to God, aloud to God, that he may hear me. In the day of my trouble I seek the Lord; in the night my hand is stretched out without wearying; my soul refuses to be comforted. I think of God, and I moan; I meditate, and my spirit faints. 'Will the Lord spurn for ever, and never again be favourable? Has his steadfast love ceased for ever? Are his promises at an end for all time?'   Psalm 77:1-3, 7-8

Hear my prayer, O Lord; let my cry come to you. Do not hide your face from me in the

day of my distress. Incline your ear to me;
answer me speedily in the day when I call.

Psalm 102:1-2

You're here, Lord!
How did I never see it before?
How did I go so long,
    aching,
    thirsting,
    searching,
    when all the time you were here,
    standing by my side,
    right before my very eyes?
It's astonishing, yet it's true –
    day after day I've gone through life
    oblivious to your presence.
I've knelt in prayer and begged you to hear me,
    I've shared in worship, hungry to meet you,
    I've studied your word, thirsting for guidance,
    yet when you answered,
    when you touched my soul,
    I never knew it, even when you called my name.
Why Lord?
Wasn't I listening?
Was my mind distracted,
    my attention elsewhere?
I thought I was ready,
    tuned in and waiting,
    but I wasn't,
    for somehow I missed you
    when you were there all along.

My child,
    there's no mystery,
    strange though it all seems to you.
You were listening,
    as eagerly and intently as I could have wished for,
    except for one thing –
    it was for *your* answer,
    in *your* time,
    on *your* terms!
That's what muddled you.
When I told you to wait, you wanted to hurry;
    when I answered no, you shouted yes;
    when I asked for patience,
    you chafed with frustration;
    when I urged you forward, you wandered back.
It wasn't me you were looking for,
    much though you thought it,
    but yourself –
    me made in your image
    rather than you made in mine,
    and that's why you never heard.
But I was there for all that,
    just as I always am,
    just as I'll always be,
    speaking my word,
    leading you by the hand,
    offering you my guidance,
    and waiting till you respond.
So the next time you do not see me,
    when you call my name
    and I do not seem to answer,

look within and ask yourself:
are you really listening,
and do you want to hear?

*Where can I go from your spirit? Or where can I
flee from your presence? If I ascend to heaven,
you are there; if I make my bed in Sheol, you
are there. If I take the wings of the morning and
settle at the farthest limits of the sea, even there
your hand shall lead me, and your right hand
shall hold me fast.* Psalm 139:7-10

25

I've got it all planned

Even the best laid plans, so they say, go to waste. Yet it is in the nature of humankind to plan ahead. We want to know what life has in store. We feel the need for a clear sense of direction. And we do everything in our power to ensure the future measures up to our expectations. There is no shortage of encouragement to such a way of thinking. Pension firms urge us to plan for retirement; insurance companies offer cover against each and every eventuality; banks and building societies offer us all manner of investment schemes which promise bumper tax-free pay-outs ten, fifteen, twenty-five years into the future. All, of course, have their place, for those who can afford them, as part of a sensible stewardship of their resources, but neither these nor anything else can guarantee the future. We never know what tomorrow may bring. While it is necessary in life to look ahead, it is also vital to live each day as it comes, valuing it for what it is, and being open to what it may bring.

All our steps are ordered by the Lord; how then can we understand our own ways?
Proverbs 20:24

Do not boast about tomorrow, for you do not know what a day may bring. Proverbs 27:1

Come now, you who say, 'Today or tomorrow we will go to such and such a town and spend a year there, doing business and making money.' Yet you do not even know what tomorrow will bring. What is your life? For you are a mist that appears for a little while and then vanishes. Instead you ought to say, 'If the Lord wishes, we will live and do this or that.' James 4:13-15

I've got it all planned, Lord,
    down to the very last detail,
    everything mapped out just as I want it to be.
And it's marvellous to know at long last where I stand,
    to have a clear idea of where I'm going
    and what I want.
It's been a long time coming –
    for most of my life I've just drifted along
    with no sense of purpose
    and little hope for the future,
    content simply to get by as best I can,
    avoiding the pitfalls,
    making the best of the good times,
    holding on through the bad.
Even when I had a clearer picture –
    a vision to work towards,
    a dream to aim for –
    all too often that was thwarted,

life twisting and turning,
wriggling off the line,
just when I thought I had it under control.
But suddenly it's all changed,
everything finally slotting into place,
and this time Lord it will be different:
no mistakes,
no letting the prize slip through my fingers –
I know what I want,
and I'm going to reach out to make it mine.

My child,
what are you saying?
After all you've been through,
you know life's not that simple.
I'm glad you're excited,
for it's good to look forward,
to dream dreams,
to have hopes,
but don't get carried away,
or you'll fall over yourself in your hurry.
You can't control the future;
it's in my hands –
and if that's hard to live with sometimes,
not knowing what the next day might bring,
ask yourself this:
would you really want it any different?
You may think so,
but consider the responsibility involved,
the decisions to be taken,

the choices to be made,
each affecting not just you
but the lives of those around you.
And could you know today
what you will want tomorrow,
the way your thoughts might change,
your tastes evolve,
your aspirations alter as the years go by?
I doubt it,
but, assuming you could,
just imagine a life with no surprises,
closed to the unexpected,
everything running precisely to plan –
is that how you'd like to live?
No, my child, it's not you who holds the future,
it's me;
and though you may wish it were different,
though it's hard sometimes to accept,
there's nowhere better to leave it.

*You turn us back to dust, and say, 'Turn back,
you mortals.' For a thousand years in your sight
are like yesterday when it is past, or like a watch
in the night. You sweep them away; they are
like a dream, like grass that is renewed in the
morning; in the morning it flourishes and is
renewed; in the evening it fades and withers.*
Psalm 90:3-6

I know, O Lord, that the way of human beings is not in their control, that mortals as they walk cannot direct their steps.   Jeremiah 10:23

The plans of the mind belong to mortals, but the answer of the tongue is from the Lord. The human mind plans the way, but the Lord directs the steps.   Proverbs 16:1, 9

The human mind may devise many plans, but it is the purpose of the Lord that will be established.   Proverbs 19:21

26

Lord, I sent a card today

I have often been struck by how much people will do for a simple 'thank you'. In almost all of us there is a craving for appreciation, the need to feel valued and worth something. A simple expression of gratitude can mean as much as any material inducement, spurring us to new efforts and greater heights. Yet, sadly, where it matters, 'thank you' is all too rarely said. The multitude of little tasks done for us day by day, the gestures of service behind the scenes, the unsung contributions to our lives, more often than not pass unnoticed, unrecognised. And I suspect the same is true in our dealings with God. If you are anything like me, your prayers are long on 'please' and short on 'thank you'. There is so much we want God to do for us, so many requests we bombard him with, but when our prayers are answered, how many times, I wonder, do we make a point of showing our appreciation?

It is good to give thanks to the Lord, to sing praises to your name, O Most High; to declare your steadfast love in the morning, and your faithfulness by night. For you, O Lord, have made me glad by your work; at the works of your hands I sing for joy. Psalm 92:1-2, 4

Lord, I sent a card today.
Nothing out of the ordinary,
    just a simple thank-you note for a special gift.
There was no need to send it,
    for it wasn't expected,
    and I very nearly didn't, time,
    as always, being short.
But that present had meant something to me,
    touched my heart,
    and I wanted to show my appreciation,
    to make it plain it wasn't just taken for granted,
    but that I was truly grateful.
Yet it struck me, Lord,
    as I popped that card into the post-box,
    that while I'm good on the whole
    at saying thank you to others,
    I'm pretty hopeless when it comes to you.
I'd never considered it before,
    the thought simply not occurring to me,
    but suddenly I realised my prayers
    are all too often 'please'
    and all too rarely 'thank you'.
It's true, isn't it, Lord?
I'm always after something –
    another problem to be solved,
    another request,
    another need,
    another desire –
    and I bring them to you without a second thought,
    almost automatically,
    confident you'll help.

But when the crisis is over,
    your answer given,
    it's all forgotten,
    nothing more said until the next time.
There's no excuse, Lord, I know that –
    so today, quite simply, I want to say thank you,
    thank you, for everything.

My child,
    thank *you*.
It's good to hear you,
    for, believe me, you're not the only one
    who fails to thank me.
I'm inundated each day by a multitude of people
    with a multitude of requests,
    a myriad of problems –
    yet a modicum of gratitude.
'Do this', they tell me,
    'Do that',
    'Give me strength',
    'Hear my prayer'.
And I do,
    willingly,
    only too glad to grant my blessing.
I don't demand a response or even expect one,
    love bringing its own reward,
    but to know I've touched a life and given joy
    means as much to me as it would to anyone.
In fact, there's only one thing more special,
    and that's when someone not only says thank you

but shows they mean it –
responding when I offer guidance,
trusting when I offer strength,
risking when I offer freedom,
rejoicing when I offer life.
Do that, my child –
show gratitude in action –
and words no longer matter,
for it's all the thanks I need.

Enter his gates with thanksgiving, and his courts with praise. Give thanks to him, bless his name. For the Lord is good; his steadfast love endures for ever, and his faithfulness to all generations. Psalm 100:4-5

Be filled with the Spirit, as you sing psalms and hymns and spiritual songs among yourselves, singing and making melody to the Lord in your hearts, giving thanks to God the Father at all times and for everything in the name of our Lord Jesus Christ. Ephesians 5:18b-20

Do not worry about anything, but in everything by prayer and supplication with thanksgiving let your requests be made known to God.
Philippians 4:6

27

Which way now, Lord?

There was a song in the charts many years ago now with the title 'Torn between two lovers' – a powerful ballad about a woman caught between two equally passionate attachments. Hopefully, most of us will be spared facing a dilemma quite as traumatic as that, but life nonetheless has a habit of throwing up situations which involve the making of difficult choices. Sometimes the options before us are equally attractive; on other occasions we may have to choose between the lesser of two evils – but eventually a decision has to be taken. We cannot live a double life, nor can we sit on the fence and have the best of both worlds.

Sometimes there is a way that seems to be right, but in the end it is the way to death.
                                    Proverbs 16:25

Which way now, Lord?
I have to ask, for I'm lost,
    confused,
    uncertain of the way forward.
You see, I'm torn between two choices –
    my heart saying one thing,

but my head another –
and I can't make up my mind which to listen to,
which way I ought to take.
It's not that one is wrong and the other right –
if that were the case there would be no problem,
the decision as good as made.
But they both have points in their favour,
and points against,
their share of good,
and their share of bad.
I ought to make up my mind, I know that,
yet I don't want to,
for I'm afraid of missing out,
of regretting my decision
and wishing I could put the clock back
and try again.
So forgive me, Lord,
but unless you're willing
to show me the way forward,
unmistakably,
beyond all possibility of misunderstanding,
I'm going to hedge my bets,
and sit on the fence,
for as long as it's possible to stay there.

My child,
don't do that, please.
I understand your quandary,
for it is hard to choose
when your future is in the balance,

when the decision you make
may change your very life.
I want to help you,
and I'll do all I can,
but I can't give you the answer,
for it's your life we're talking about here,
not mine,
and until you've faced the questions raised
and worked the issues through,
no answer will make sense fully.
But I tell you this:
although a foot in both camps
may seem attractive,
don't be fooled –
it will lead to disaster.
For in trying to serve two masters
you will serve neither,
and in seeking the best of both worlds
you will feel out of place in each.
So take your time,
weigh up the options,
and then decide.
And having done that, look forward,
not backwards,
to the future, not the past,
for, though an option may be lost,
true peace will be gained.

Now if you are unwilling to serve the Lord, choose this day whom you will serve . . . but as for me and my household, we will serve the Lord.   Joshua 24:15

Desire without knowledge is not good, and one who moves too hurriedly misses the way.
                                                        Proverbs 19:2

No one can serve two masters; for a slave will either hate the one and love the other or be devoted to the one and despise the other.
                                                        Matthew 6:24

28

I picked up the paper

Since childhood I have always been fascinated by words. There is something almost awesome about the way a gifted speaker can capture the imagination of their audience, or the way a skilful writer can transport a reader into another world simply through words on a page. The pen is indeed mightier than the sword. But, like all good things, there is a negative side to this truth, words all too easily being used to hurt and destroy, cheat and deceive, ridicule or revile. We will all be able to recall times when we opened our mouths without stopping to think, or when we spoke cruelly, intent on wounding. We will all have encountered people who never stop talking, wearing us out with their incessant, empty chatter. And we will all be aware of the way words have been used to incite hatred and intolerance, violence and war. Words are God's gift, but they are a gift that needs to be handled with care, recognising their potential for good or evil.

When words are many, transgression is not lacking, but the prudent are restrained in speech.
Proverbs 10:19

The words of the mouth are deep waters; the fountain of wisdom is a gushing stream. A fool's lips bring strife, and a fool's mouth invites a flogging. The mouths of fools are their ruin, and their lips a snare to themselves. The words of a whisperer are like delicious morsels; they go down into the inner parts of the body.
Proverbs 18:4, 6-8

I picked up the paper, Lord,
    and the words leapt out at me –
    loud,
    strident,
    provocative,
    demanding my attention,
    dictating my thoughts.
And I glimpsed suddenly
    the enormous power of words,
    a power both wonderful and terrifying.
We need them, Lord, I know that,
    for where would we be without them?
Yet they're a mystery,
    a curious enigma,
    capable of so much good yet so much evil,
    so much beauty yet so much ugliness.
We can speak to heal, or wound,
    to bless, or curse,
    to encourage, or scold,
    to build up, or destroy –
    one word able to lift our spirits

or break our hearts,
to reveal the truth or keep it hidden.
It's sobering, Lord,
almost frightening,
for it brings home
the awesome yet chilling responsibility
this gift entails,
the realisation that every time I open my mouth
or pick up my pen
I handle a two-edged sword.
Lord, teach me to think first and speak second,
and grant that what I say, the words I use,
may be acceptable in your sight.

My child,
you have spoken to me,
and I have listened,
hearing your prayer
with open ear and ready heart,
for it's true what you say –
one word so sweet yet so sour,
so rich yet so poor.
I know it all too well,
for I watch day by day
as words are thrown around
like so much rubbish –
tossed casually in careless chatter,
hurled with venom in bitter abuse,
twisted beyond recognition in idle gossip.
I hear words of mockery, scorn and prejudice,

of hatred, bitterness and violence,
and I grieve to see a gift so precious
turned into something so cheap.
Yet it's no good just talking – I realise that:
we must act as well as speak
if we would be heard –
so I came among you,
the Word made flesh,
demonstrating my love,
showing mercy,
bestowing life.
I spoke, my child,
and I go on speaking,
through a bloodstained cross,
and an empty tomb,
through a broken Saviour, and a risen Lord,
not demanding your attention,
but inviting your response,
not controlling your thoughts,
but renewing your minds.
So listen to me,
give ear to my voice,
and you will hear Good News,
tidings to bring joy to your soul
and praise to your lips –
I give you my word.

Rash words are like sword thrusts, but the tongue of the wise brings healing.

Proverbs 12:18

The Word became flesh and lived among us, and we have seen his glory, the glory as of a father's only son, full of grace and truth.

John 1:14

Let your speech always be gracious, seasoned with salt, so that you may know how you ought to answer everyone. Colossians 4:6

Anyone who makes no mistakes in speaking is perfect, able to keep the whole body in check with a bridle. If we put bits into the mouths of horses to make them obey us, we guide their whole bodies. Or look at ships: though they are so large that it takes strong winds to drive them, yet they are guided by a very small rudder wherever the will of the pilot directs. So also the tongue is a small member, yet it boasts of great exploits. No one can tame the tongue – a restless evil, full of deadly poison. With it we bless the Lord and Father, and with it we curse those who are made in the likeness of God. From the same mouth come blessing and cursing. My brothers and sisters, this ought not to be so.

James 3:2-5, 8-10

29

One day, Lord

Of the three great Christian gifts spoken of by the Apostle Paul in his first letter to the Corinthians, the most neglected is surely hope. We hear much in the Church of faith and love, but hope seems to be the poor relation, seldom getting much of a mention and probably rarely even thought of as a gift at all. Yet what would life be without it? The very idea is unthinkable. Not hope in the sense of wishful thinking – that is simply an illusion. Nor clinging to a last shred of conviction in what we might call hoping against hope – that is plain foolishness. No, the hope which God gives us is a confidence in the future based upon the present experience of his love – a conviction that, whatever happens, Christ will be with us just as he is with us now. We do not know the precise details of what that future holds, nor do we need to know. We have the assurance that God is at work in our lives, and one day his purpose will be fulfilled. What more could we want?

Why are you cast down, O my soul, and why are you disquieted within me? Hope in God; for I shall again praise him, my help and my God.
Psalm 42:5-6a

*For God alone my soul waits in silence, for my
hope is from him. He alone is my rock and my
salvation, my fortress; I shall not be shaken.*
                                        Psalm 62:5-6

*Hope deferred makes the heart sick, but a
desire fulfilled is a tree of life.*   Proverbs 13:12

One day, Lord, that's what I tell myself –
    one day the clouds will lift and the sun shine,
    the rain stop and the birds sing.
I don't know when and I don't know how,
    but I hold on to that conviction day after day,
    a constant source of strength in the storms of life.
Yet, it's hard sometimes, I have to admit it –
    when fears come true,
    and dreams prove false;
    when knocks mount up,
    and life gets me down –
    it's hard not to question,
    to fear that hope's in vain.
And if that's not enough,
    I look around at our troubled world –
    its hatred, violence, greed and envy,
    its injustice, corruption, indifference and apathy –
    and yes, Lord,
    there are times when I almost stop believing.
Almost, but not quite,
    for I have tasted your love
    and glimpsed your purpose,

I've felt your power and known your grace;
and you have woken my soul
to a new kind of living,
a new kind of world,
a hope worth waiting for.
One day, Lord,
one day the sun will shine.

My child,
keep looking,
keep hoping,
keep praying,
keep trusting,
for it will happen, just as you say.
However hard it may be,
however foolish it may seem,
hold on to the faith you have now,
the conviction that my will shall be done.
For though life is dark and the future looks bleak,
though good seems destroyed and evil triumphant,
the light will continue to shine
and nothing will overcome it.
There's much that conspires against me,
much which frustrates my purpose
and obscures my love,
but the time is coming
when the poor will be rich and the hungry fed,
the deaf hear and the blind see,
the dumb speak and the lame walk,
the sick be healed and the dead raised.

It may be sooner, it may be later,
   it may seem near, it may seem far,
   but come rain or sunshine,
   storm or calm,
   I shall be patiently building my kingdom,
   until it comes to pass.
So don't lose heart, my child, whatever happens –
   trust in me and believe in the future,
   for when you lose hope, you lose all.

We boast in our hope of sharing the glory of God. And not only that, but we also boast in our sufferings, knowing that suffering produces endurance, and endurance produces character, and character produces hope, and hope does not disappoint us, because God's love has been poured into our hearts through the Holy Spirit that has been given to us.   Romans 5:2b-5

In hope we were saved. Now hope that is seen is not hope. For who hopes for what is seen? But if we hope for what we do not see, we wait for it with patience.   Romans 8:24-25

Now faith is the assurance of things hoped for, the conviction of things not seen.   Hebrews 11:1

30

'Don't make me laugh,' he said

Towards the end of my ministry in Cheltenham I organised a special if rather unusual service – a celebration of laughter. We had held music services and songs of praise services, so, I decided, why not a laughter service? And through a carefully chosen selection of jokes, sketches, anecdotes and humorous stories, together with a clip from a Mr Bean video, we thanked God for the ability to laugh. Why not, for surely the Christian life above all should be about joy? Yet the idea of worship including fun and of Christians having a sense of humour struck many people as odd – so much so that the service made it into the pages of a national newspaper and earned me a live telephone interview on Radio Newcastle, not to mention a sharp letter in a local paper condemning my blasphemous and heretical idea! Is the idea of God enjoying a good joke so shocking? I hope not, for heaven will be a dull place if it is!

When the Lord restored the fortunes of Zion, we were like those who dream. Then our mouth was filled with laughter, and our tongue with shouts of joy; then it was said among the nations, 'The Lord has done great things for

them.' The Lord has done great things for us,
and we rejoiced.   Psalm 126:1-3

There is a time to weep, and a time to laugh;
a time to mourn, and a time to dance.
                                    Ecclesiastes 3:4

'Don't make me laugh,' he said.
And I knew what he meant,
    for I've said it often enough myself.
But today, Lord, I'm asking the opposite –
    make me laugh, please,
    for of all your gifts
    there is none more precious than laughter.
Not the laughter of mockery – I don't mean that –
    jeering at someone in their misfortune,
    but the ability to laugh *with* the world
    and *at* myself –
    to greet life with a smile,
    a wry grin,
    seeing the funny side
    of even the darkest moments;
    serious when I have to be,
    but recognising the foolish,
    the absurd and comical,
    and sharing the joke with you.
Teach me that, Lord,
    give me the wisdom,
    the confidence,
    the faith,

and the humility,
to look at the solemnity and the tragedy of life,
and yet see the wonderful humour within.

My child,
thank you for your prayer,
for seeing me as I am
rather than as I'm so often painted.
It gladdens my spirit to hear you,
for all too many regard me as solemn and sombre,
a tight-lipped, po-faced God,
with never a smile or chuckle crossing my lips.
I understand why,
for I can be stern,
even forbidding,
the issues I raise and the challenge I bring
no laughing matter.
And there are times when what passes as humour
fills me with sadness –
the cruel jibe,
the sick joke,
the heartless teasing,
the cutting sarcasm.
But there's another side also,
a part of me that revels in laughter
and loves to see a smile on your faces,
that delights in fun and longs to share it with you,
for I know that happiness breeds happiness,
and cheer spreads cheer,
joy aids healing, and sunshine brings life.

So yes, there's a time to weep, but also to laugh,
    a time to mourn, but also to dance,
    and if you lose that balance,
    it's serious indeed,
    for I fear you've lost sight of me.

He will yet fill your mouth with laughter, and your lips with shouts of joy.   Job 8:21

A glad heart makes a cheerful countenance, but by sorrow of heart the spirit is broken. All the days of the poor are hard, but a cheerful heart has a continual feast.   Proverbs 15:13, 15

A cheerful heart is a good medicine, but a downcast spirit dries up the bones.
    Proverbs 17:22

Blessed are you who weep now, for you will laugh.   Luke 6:21b

Rejoice in the Lord always; again I will say, Rejoice.   Philippians 4:4

31

Lord, I had it coming to me

When does virtue become a vice? That is a question one might well ask when considering the subject of pride. There is a sense in which to be proud is a good thing – we all need a proper pride in ourselves, our work and our achievements, and without that we would be sorry people indeed. Yet there are few individuals more objectionable than those who are puffed up with their own importance, those who look disapprovingly down their noses at those around them. Such people, as the old proverb reminds us, are inevitably heading for an unpleasant, but fully deserved, fall.

Pride goes before destruction, and a haughty spirit before a fall. It is better to be of a lowly spirit among the poor than to divide the spoil with the proud. Proverbs 16:18-19

Let another praise you, and not your own mouth – a stranger, and not your own lips.
Proverbs 27:2

Lord, I had it coming to me,
    for I was so full of myself,
    so ready to thrust myself forward.
Oh, I disguised it, of course,
    assuming a veil of modesty,
    but I longed to be in the limelight,
    to have the stage all to myself.
'Look at me!' – that's what I was saying –
    'Look what I've done!'
    'Aren't I the clever one?'
And the sad thing is after a time I almost believed it,
    my little world becoming all important,
    and my small achievements put before any others.
I should have listened – I realise that now –
    paid heed to that wise old proverb:
    'Pride goes before a fall.'
But I didn't,
    and I've come down to earth with a vengeance,
    my face rubbed in the dust.
It hurts to admit it, Lord,
    to let go of the illusion,
    but I had it coming, and it serves me right,
    for I thought I was something special,
    and I couldn't have been more mistaken.

My child,
    steady now –
    let's keep things in perspective.
You *were* too full of yourself,
    and I'm glad the bubble has been pricked,

for there are few things more ugly than conceit.
But don't put yourself down – that will help no one.
You *are* special, because I made you –
    a unique individual with your own gifts,
    your own talents,
    your own qualities.
And you have as much worth,
    as much to contribute, as the next person.
But that has two sides, doesn't it?
For that next person is special too,
    with as much to be proud of,
    as good a reason to boast,
    as anyone.
So think highly of yourself,
    and highly of others;
    rejoice in your gifts,
    rejoice also in theirs –
    and then there'll be no more putting you down;
    just me lifting you up.

For by the grace given to me I say to everyone among you not to think of yourself more highly than you ought to think, but to think with sober judgement, each according to the measure of faith that God has assigned.   Romans 12:3

Consider your own call, brothers and sisters: not many of you were wise by human standards, not many were powerful, not many were of noble birth. But God chose what is foolish in the world to shame the wise; God chose what is weak in the world to shame the strong; God chose what is low and despised in the world, things that are not, to reduce to nothing things that are, so that no one might boast in the presence of God. He is the source of your life in Christ Jesus, who became for us wisdom from God, and righteousness and sanctification and redemption, in order that, as it is written, 'Let the one who boasts, boast in the Lord.'   1 Corinthians 1:26-31

Do nothing from selfish ambition or conceit, but in humility regard others as better than yourselves.   Philippians 2:3

Humble yourselves therefore under the mighty hand of God, so that he may exalt you in due time.   1 Peter 5:6

_____ 32 _____
If only I'd known

When I was training for the ministry at college there was a certain poster very much in vogue among my colleagues. It was a cartoon depicting four cows in adjoining fields, each leaning over their neighbour's fence to munch the grass in their field. And the caption? Well, there was no need for one, was there? A delightful illustration of that old saying about the grass always being greener on the other side. And illusory though that greener grass may be, it is so true of the way we think. Instead of being content with what we have, we just can't help looking jealously at those around us, eyeing up their latest acquisition, their comfortable lifestyle, their beautiful house, and wishing it was ours. A daily bombardment of advertising wards off any possibility of us coming to our senses. Occasionally, of course, the grass is greener, in material terms anyway. But if we allow ourselves to get sucked into the whirlpool of envy, then the quality of our lives will spiral downwards, for in time our view of everything and everyone will be contaminated by its poison.

Wrath is cruel, anger is overwhelming, but who is able to stand before jealousy?   Proverbs 27:4

There are many who say, 'O that we might see some good! Let the light of your face shine on us, O Lord!' You have put gladness in my heart more than when their grain and wine abound.

Psalm 4:6-7

If only I'd known, Lord,
    if I'd had even the slightest inkling,
    I would have thought and acted so differently.
But I'd no idea, that was the trouble,
    I looked at the outside
    and saw the things they had which I didn't –
    the nice house,
    the new car,
    the latest gadgets,
    the smart clothes –
    and I was jealous, no point pretending.
They had everything, Lord,
    that's how it seemed –
    you name it, it was theirs,
    and it just seemed so unfair,
    so unjust –
    I simply couldn't get it out of my mind.
I'd been happy until then –
    that's what makes it so stupid –
    quite content with my lot,
    but suddenly it all changed,
    envy seeping like poison deep within,
    eating away inside,
    destroying my very soul.

And the irony is I was mistaken,
    for they didn't bring happiness, those possessions –
    far from it –
    they were a flimsy veneer
    disguising a loveless relationship,
    a bitter separation,
    a broken family.
It needn't have been like that, of course,
    but it was,
    and what shames me most
    is that I never even considered the possibility.
I should have looked more closely, Lord,
    seen beneath the surface to the reality below.
But I tell you what, Lord –
    it taught me something, that experience:
    it taught me to count my blessings,
    to realise how lucky I am
    and how much I have to thank you for;
    it taught me to look at the good things in life,
    the innumerable blessings
    and countless joys there are to celebrate;
    it taught me to appreciate everything
    I have received,
    and live each day as your gift.
Forgive me, Lord, for not seeing it before.
Forgive me for being so concerned
    with what I hadn't got
    that I failed to recognise all you'd given.

My child,
    you've begun to see life differently,
    and I'm glad,
    not just for my sake, but yours,
    for you were wasting life,
    throwing away all I so wanted you to enjoy.
It's good to see you happy again,
    celebrating as you ought to,
    but now you've started, don't stop,
    for it's all too easy to slip back into old habits.
I see it happen all the time,
    one moment a gift seeming wonderful,
    and the next dulled by familiarity,
    one day prayers offered to me
    in joyful thanksgiving,
    the next in bitter complaint.
You think you've changed,
    and I know you mean to,
    but don't be complacent,
    for it's a subtle thing, envy,
    like a pernicious weed
    lurking in the crevices of your mind,
    waiting to catch you unawares.
It doesn't take much,
    just the briefest of glimpses,
    and the seeds shoot again,
    suffocating happiness,
    destroying peace.
Remember that, my child:
    rejoice in all I've given
    and you will find contentment.

Keep on counting your blessings,
today and every day,
and you will find them too many to number,
your cup running over with good things.

As long as there is jealousy and quarrelling among you, are you not of the flesh, and behaving according to human inclinations?
1 Corinthians 3:3

Be content with what you have. Hebrews 13:5

Who is wise and understanding among you? Show by your good life that your works are done with gentleness born of wisdom. But if you have bitter envy and selfish ambition in your hearts, do not be boastful and false to the truth. Such wisdom does not come down from above, but is earthly, unspiritual, devilish. For where there is envy and selfish ambition, there will also be disorder and wickedness of every kind. James 3:13-16

33

It was such a let-down, Lord

There is an old saying, 'It is better to have loved and lost than never to have loved at all', and I've no doubt that is true. But to experience joy and then to lose it, or to have high hopes only to have them dashed, can be a bitterly painful experience. Disappointment can be a crushing emotion, for a time blotting out all else. Indeed, there can come a point when any ability to believe in the future is extinguished altogether, so powerful is the fear of being hurt once again. Yet the Christian Gospel at its heart is about the resurrection of broken lives, broken dreams, broken confidence – the assurance that the darkest, bleakest moments can be transformed into a gateway to new life and opportunity.

Why are you cast down, O my soul, and why are you disquieted within me? Hope in God; for I shall again praise him, my help and my God.
Psalm 42:5

I considered all that my hands had done and the toil I had spent in doing it, and again, all was vanity and a chasing after wind, and there was nothing to be gained under the sun.
Ecclesiastes 2:11

He has made my teeth grind on gravel, and made me cower in ashes; my soul is bereft of peace; I have forgotten what happiness is; so I say, 'Gone is my glory, and all that I had hoped for from the Lord.'   Lamentations 3:16-18

It was such a let-down, Lord,
    after all the build-up and anticipation,
    such a dreadful disappointment –
    like a long-awaited flower failing to open,
    a prize bloom scorched by the frost –
    a poignant reminder of what might have been.
And I was so looking forward,
    almost tingling with anticipation
    as the moment drew near.
It was to change my life,
    to answer all my prayers,
    everything at last as I wanted it to be.
Was that too much to ask?
Well, yes, maybe it was unrealistic to put it mildly,
    yet I dared to dream, Lord,
    I dared to hold a vision of the future,
    for I thought that's what you expect of us,
    what faith is all about.
I was mistaken – I must have been –
    for look at me now:
    my hopes in tatters,
    my dreams in ruins,
    but I don't know why,
    where I went so wrong,

and the one thing I can't help asking is,
if you had to let me down,
couldn't it have been more gently?

My child,
I'm sorry, truly I am,
for it grieves me to see you feeling like this,
so disillusioned and miserable.
But it's not me who failed you – don't think that –
it's the things you put your faith in.
You were right to look forward –
it *is* what I want and where faith should lead,
but to pin all your hopes on one moment,
to put all your trust in one person –
that was asking for trouble,
setting yourself up for a disappointment,
for there is nothing and no one,
no matter how special,
who can answer all your prayers.
Don't think I'm being dismissive,
for I would never be that, not of anyone –
you may find great joy,
you may share deep love,
but there will always be that space in your life
which I alone can fill.
And I *will* fill it, my child,
brimming to overflowing
if you put your faith in me –
though all else fail you, I will not.
So dream your dreams and see your visions,

only this time build them on me,
and not this world,
for then, I promise, you won't be disappointed.

*Happy are those whose help is the God of
Jacob, whose hope is in the Lord their God.*
                                                    Psalm 146:5

*Now faith is the assurance of things hoped for,
the conviction of things not seen.*   Hebrews 11:1

34

It was the last straw

Few of us in our lives will be fortunate enough to escape being badly let down or hurt by someone. A close relationship may end in acrimony; a trusted friend betray a confidence; a broken promise deny us a long-dreamed-of opportunity; or a moment's carelessness wreck our lives. How do we cope with such experiences? There are two options – either we face them for what they are, working through the pain until we finally come to terms with it; or we can dwell on the injustice of life, licking our wounds and wallowing in self-pity. The latter reaction is perfectly understandable but ultimately tragic, for it succeeds only in adding insult to injury, robbing life of its joy and beauty. There are few people more lonely than those who are bitter in spirit.

I will not restrain my mouth; I will speak in the anguish of my spirit; I will complain in the bitterness of my soul. Job 7:11

The heart knows its own bitterness, and no stranger shares its joy. Proverbs 14:10

It was the last straw, Lord –
    they were broken,
    scarred in spirit,
    the light gone from their eyes.
And I could see why, all too clearly,
    for life had been cruel,
    harsh in the extreme,
    sucking them slowly dry.
It hadn't been just one disappointment –
    they could have lived with that, shrugged it off –
    but they had known many,
    time and again hope beckoning them forward
    only to knock them backwards.
They'd tried even then,
    putting a brave face on for the world,
    but the smile had worn thin
    as the blows kept coming –
    another chance missed,
    another ambition thwarted,
    another dream crushed,
    another failure to live with.
It hurt me to see them, Lord,
    so bitter and twisted,
    so angry at life,
    but I couldn't blame them,
    still less condemn,
    for I know in their shoes I'd have felt just the same.
Lord, save me from that –
    teach me to meet life's blows with cheerfulness,
    to face defeat with dignity,
    to see hopes crushed,

trust broken,
and love betrayed,
yet still carry light in my soul.

My child,
    remember this moment,
    the pain you've seen,
    the scars inflicted,
    and remember the prayer you offered.
For life will bring hurt, whoever you are,
    its share of hardship and sorrow,
    and, though you try to meet them cheerfully,
    such times will take their toll.
I've seen it happen all too often –
    an opportunity wasted,
    a hope denied,
    a desire frustrated –
    and suddenly regrets take over,
    festering inside,
    until there is nothing left
    but dull and bitter resentment.
Don't think I condemn, any more than you do,
    for they have reason to be angry
    and cause to complain,
    but it hurts me, more than I can say,
    to see a heart starved,
    and a soul shrivelled,
    poisoned by its own gall.
And it can happen, my child,
    to you as much as anyone –

if you dwell on the past and brood on your lot.
So come to me and let it all out,
before what might have been
destroys what yet can be.

*Put away from you all bitterness and wrath and
anger and wrangling and slander, together with
all malice, and be kind to one another, tender-
hearted, forgiving one another, as God in Christ
has forgiven you.*　　　　　Ephesians 4:31-32

*See to it that no one fails to obtain the grace of
God; that no root of bitterness springs up and
causes trouble, and through it many become
defiled.*　　　　　Hebrews 12:15

35

I saw the advert

'Buy now, pay later.' Visit almost any retail store you care to mention and the chances are you will see an offer very similar to that. We live in an age of easy credit, an age in which people are encouraged to spend, regardless of the consequences. If you want it, we are told, have it now – why wait? Yet the promise of instant satisfaction proves illusory, for once let loose the desire to have more takes over, its appetite devouring all in its path. It is hardly surprising that greed is listed as one of the seven deadly sins, for there are few vices more destructive of both self and others.

The greedy person stirs up strife, but whoever trusts in the Lord will be enriched.

Proverbs 28:25

I saw the advert, Lord,
    calling out to me from the hoarding,
    bold,
    brash,
    yet subtly persuasive –
    the same picture I'd seen on the television,
    at the cinema,

in the magazine,
with the same extravagant promise,
the same dramatic claims:
new,
bigger,
faster,
better.
Was it true?
It might have been,
   and it might not.
But standing before that poster
   I realised the question was irrelevant,
   for it wasn't the facts here that mattered,
   nor on truth that sales were pitched,
   but the desire to have more –
   the smartest model,
   the latest craze,
   the newest gadget –
   always one thing more
   enticing us to worship at the altar of greed.
I saw it, Lord,
   and I hung my head,
   for I knew it wasn't just others this was aimed at,
   the grasping world out there –
   it was me,
   for in my own way I'm as guilty,
   as greedy,
   as any.

My child,
    you've seen through the sales talk,
    behind the façade,
    to the truth that really matters,
    and it's good you have,
    for greed will destroy you,
    poison your very soul.
But now you've seen it, I have to ask you:
    what now,
    what difference does it make?
There are plenty who acknowledge their greed,
    few who curb their appetites.
There are many who decry materialism,
    a handful who live more simply.
Yet that's what matters –
    whether your words lead to actions,
    your theory to practice.
You can confess as often as you like,
    but unless you want to change,
    and unless you try to do so,
    your penitence is hollow,
    vain talk counting for nothing.
And the tragedy is it's not just you who suffers –
    it's others,
    those who have so little
    because you have so much.
That treat you bought yourself today,
    that little extra –
    you didn't need it,
    scarcely even wanted it,
    but the money you spent –

what a difference it could have made to others!
That latest purchase of yours,
    that new acquisition –
    it may please you for a while,
    but it will never satisfy,
    another fancy soon to take its place;
    yet, for what it cost you, a child goes hungry.
And so it goes on,
    the more you have, the more you seek,
    whilst those with little have even less.
That's the reality,
    the price of greed,
    a broken world where some are full,
    yet all are empty.
So next time you see that advert,
    don't hang your head, for that won't help.
Try shaking it instead,
    saying no to self,
    and let enough be enough.

*My child, if sinners entice you, do not consent
. . . do not walk in their way, keep your foot
from their paths. They lie in wait – to kill
themselves! – and set an ambush – for their
own lives! Such is the end of all who are
greedy for gain; it takes away the life of its
possessors.*   Proverbs 1:10, 15, 18-19

*I have learned to be content with whatever I
have. I know what it is to have little, and I know*

what it is to have plenty. In any and all circum-stances I have learned the secret of being well-fed and of going hungry, of having plenty and of being in need.   Philippians 4:11-12

___ 36 ___
It was beautiful

One of the wonderful things about life is its constant ability to surprise us. Just when we think we've seen it all, an experience comes along that leaves us gasping in astonishment, undreamt-of horizons suddenly opened to us. And it's not only the unfamiliar which has this power to amaze – it can equally often be the ordinary, everyday things of life, known to us so well that we've come to take them for granted. Suddenly they can take on a wholly unsuspected dimension, to the eye of faith speaking of God – the song of a bird, the cry of a baby, the sight of a rainbow, the pattern of a snowflake, the sound of the sea, or perhaps the simple beauty of a flower.

Consider the lilies of the field, how they grow; they neither toil nor spin, yet I tell you, even Solomon in all his glory was not clothed like one of these.   Matthew 6:28-29

O Lord, how manifold are your works! In wisdom you have made them all; the earth is full of your creatures.   Psalm 104:24

It was beautiful, Lord,
    more lovely than I'd ever begun to realise –
    a single rose,
    newly opened,
    still wet with the morning dew –
    and I stood there gazing,
    utterly enchanted by its simple perfection.
Another flower – that's how I'd seen it before –
    pleasant enough,
    attractive,
    yet hardly wonderful.
But now, as I stooped to view it closely,
    as I caught its perfume
    and noted each delicate petal,
    I glimpsed a miracle,
    a work of art,
    an astonishing labour of love.
And I saw you there, Lord,
    your hand,
    your presence –
    the gentleness of your touch,
    the order of your mind,
    the tenderness of your heart.
I saw your love expressed in that one fragile bloom,
    symbol of a world put together
    with inexpressible care –
    a world full of delight,
    able to stir our imaginations and thrill our hearts,
    to move and inspire us beyond words,
    to touch our souls with a taste of heaven.

My child,
    you think it beautiful, that flower?
I'm glad, for it's meant to be,
    though all too few see it.
But if you think that's special,
    look around you at this world I've made –
    its diversity of life,
    its variety and interest,
    so endlessly complex,
    so infinitely fascinating.
Look at the sky –
    the glow of the sun,
    the twinkle of the stars,
    the vastness of the heavens.
And most of all,
    look at yourself and your fellow human beings –
    your awesome array of talents,
    your incredible potential,
    the amazing miracle of human life.
Here too is beauty,
    most astonishing of all.
In the laughter of a child and the vigour of youth,
    in the embrace of lovers and the joy of parents,
    in the experience of maturity
    and the wisdom of age,
    I am present,
    for you are all the work of my hands,
    a testimony to my purpose,
    a reminder of my never-failing love.
So look again, my child, at that simple flower,
    at the loveliness of this world,

only see there not just the wonder of me,
but the wonder of you!

*O Lord, our Sovereign, how majestic is your
name in all the earth! You have set your
glory above the heavens. When I look at your
heavens, the work of your fingers, the moon
and the stars that you have established; what
are human beings that you are mindful of
them, mortals that you care for them? Yet you
have made them a little lower than God, and
crowned them with glory and honour. You have
given them dominion over the works of your
hands; you have put all things under their feet.
O Lord, our Sovereign, how majestic is your
name in all the earth!*   Psalm 8:1, 3-6, 9

What was it all about?

When were you last involved in an argument? Probably more recently than you care to remember. Somehow, despite our best resolutions, what begins as a disagreement seems inexorably to lead on to a quarrel. There are times, of course, when argument may be justified, but just as often it is futile, the issues so hotly disputed of little or no importance. Yet once a quarrel starts, as we will all know from experience, the initial dispute is soon overtaken as exchanges become ever more bitter and the two sides involved increasingly entrenched. How many families have been divided, friendships broken and feuds started through the most trivial of disagreements? It is all too easy to be drawn into a quarrel; another matter to pick up the pieces afterwards.

Do not quarrel with anyone without cause, when no harm has been done to you.
Proverbs 3:30

After some days Paul said to Barnabas, 'Come, let us return and visit the believers in every city where we proclaimed the word of the Lord and see how they are doing.' Barnabas wanted to take with them John called Mark.

But Paul decided not to take with them one who
had deserted them in Pamphylia and had not
accompanied them in the work. The disagree-
ment became so sharp that they parted com-
pany; Barnabas took Mark with him and sailed
away to Cyprus.   Acts 15:36-39

What was it all about, Lord, can you tell me?
It seemed important at the time –
    a matter of principle,
    almost, you might have thought,
    of life and death.
So I held my ground and argued my point,
    determined to have my say.
Was that wrong, Lord?
I didn't think so –
    he had his view and I had mine,
    so why not thrash it out,
    speak our minds and clear the air?
Yet that was then,
    and this is now –
    so little gained,
    so much destroyed.
I'm not quite sure what happened,
    but tempers frayed,
    words were twisted,
    insults traded,
    and, before we knew it,
    our trivial dispute had turned to deadly earnest.
It got us nowhere, I realise that now –

we thought too little,
and said too much –
but it's too late for regrets.
However it started, the harm is done,
and our friendship finished.

My child,
you know what it was all about, don't you?
Let's be honest, this disagreement of yours,
it was nothing –
a storm in a teacup –
and with a little more sense
you'd have sorted it out,
reached common ground or agreed to differ.
But that wasn't the issue, not once you started;
it was you,
and him,
both equally to blame –
a clash of wills,
a test of strength,
each of you reluctant to lose face
and concede defeat.
You were too proud,
too stubborn,
too quick to anger,
so you dug yourselves in,
and pulled the knives out,
refusing to give ground, whatever the cost.
And now the scars are raw
and the wounds run deep –

so great a price for so small a matter.
But it's not too late –
   you can still make peace if you want to.
Yes, it will take time –
   words spoken in haste hard to undo –
   but admit your mistake, take time to say sorry,
   and you'll be surprised at the results.
So, come on,
   swallow your pride and take the initiative,
   and next time you cannot agree,
   remember this –
   it takes two to argue,
   but just one to stop it.

The beginning of strife is like letting out water; so stop before the quarrel breaks out.
Proverbs 17:14

Like somebody who takes a passing dog by the ears is one who meddles in the quarrel of another. For lack of wood the fire goes out, and where there is no whisperer quarrelling ceases. As charcoal is to hot embers and wood to fire, so is a quarrelsome person for kindling strife. Proverbs 26:17, 20-21

Avoid stupid controversies, genealogies, dissensions, and quarrels about the law, for they are unprofitable and worthless. Titus 3:9

Those conflicts and disputes among you, where do they come from? Do they not come from your cravings that are at war within you? You want something and do not have it . . . you covet something and cannot obtain it; so you engage in disputes and conflicts.

James 4:1-2

38

Well, Lord, that's it

It is one of the unpleasant but inescapable facts of life that all of us at some time will experience sorrow. I don't just mean sadness, but rather that overwhelming sense of grief which comes through enduring real tragedy. There can be many causes, but the result is much the same – life seems hollow and without purpose. It is easy at such times to despair of the future, convinced that however hard we try we will never recapture the happiness we once had. Yet the repeated testimony of Scripture is that God has a special place in his heart for all who mourn. Sorrow will never be allowed to have the last word.

How long, O Lord? Will you forget me for ever? How long will you hide your face from me? How long must I bear pain in my soul, and have sorrow in my heart all day long? How long shall my enemy be exalted over me?

Psalm 13:1-2

As a deer longs for flowing streams, so my soul longs for you, O God. My soul thirsts for God, for the living God. When shall I come and behold the face of God? My tears have

*been my food day and night, while people say
to me continually, 'Where is your God?'*
Psalm 42:1-3

*The human spirit will endure sickness; but a
broken spirit – who can bear?*   Proverbs 18:14

*Like a moth in clothing or a worm in wood,
sorrow gnaws at the human heart.*
Proverbs 25:20b

Well, Lord, that's it,
 no point pretending any more –
 it's over,
 finished,
 the end of a beautiful chapter,
 a wonderful dream.
It was good, Lord,
 while it lasted –
 I couldn't have asked for more –
 the happiest time of my life.
And all I wanted was for it to carry on,
 just as it was,
 nothing added,
 nothing taken away.
But it's gone,
 plucked from me –
 love lost,
 hope gone,
 heart broken.

Oh, I hide it, of course –
   who wouldn't?
The pain too deep to let it show.
But underneath the painted smile,
   the mirthless laugh,
   you hear my sobs,
   and see my tears.
It's over, Lord,
   nothing left to live for,
   no point pretending,
   no point in anything.

My child,
   it's not over, believe me,
   however much it feels like it.
I know life seems grim at the moment,
   everything you hoped for and trusted in
   lying in ruins,
   but if there's one thing you can be sure of,
   when all else fails,
   it's that I am still with you,
   sharing your pain and sorrow,
   giving you strength in your hour of need.
Yes, the road will be long and hard,
   and there will be times, as now,
   when you feel crushed and broken;
   but reach out to me and you will find my hand
   waiting to lift you up,
   my arms outstretched to enfold you in love.
You may not think it possible,

but one day you will look back on this moment
with a wry smile,
even perhaps a sense of gratitude,
for you will come through it the stronger,
your inner self tested by adversity,
your faith deepened through tasting
both the triumphs
and the tragedies of this world.
So keep going, my child,
trust in me, despite everything,
and leave the future to me,
for, however long the tunnel may seem,
however dark it may become,
light will dawn and joy come again.

*Weeping may linger for the night, but joy comes
with the morning. You have turned my mourning into dancing; you have taken off my sack-
cloth and clothed me with joy, so that my soul
may praise you and not be silent. O Lord my
God, I will give thanks to you for ever.*
                                        Psalm 30:5b, 11-12

*A bruised reed he will not break, and dimly
burning wick he will not quench.*   Isaiah 42:3

39

Lord, I stood by the sea today

One of the things we all need in life is a sense of purpose, a goal to aim for. We may not always attain this, but if we can get even close then we feel the effort has been worth it. But there are times when we feel that, far from being close, we are simply going round in circles and getting nowhere. A sudden setback, an unexpected obstacle, and it can seem we are back to square one, battling against insurmountable odds. Normally, once we get over our initial disappointment, we have the resilience to bounce back, but occasionally our sense of frustration is so intense that we feel like giving up altogether, abandoning our hopes once and for all. Yet it is then, more than ever, that we need the courage to persevere, pressing on despite everything which stands in our way, to turn our dreams into reality.

Vanity of vanities, says the Teacher, vanity of vanities! All is vanity. What do people gain from all the toil at which they toil under the sun. A generation goes, and a generation comes, but the earth remains for ever. All things are wearisome; more than one can express; the eye is not satisfied with seeing or

the ear filled with hearing. What has been is
what will be, and what has been done is what
will be done; there is nothing new under the
sun. I, the Teacher, when king over Israel in
Jerusalem, applied my mind to seek and to
search out by wisdom all that is done under
heaven; it is an unhappy business that God
has given to human beings to be busy with. I
saw all the deeds that are done under the sun;
and see, all is vanity and a chasing after wind.

Ecclesiastes 1:2-4, 8-9, 12-14

Lord, I stood by the sea today,
    and I watched the waves rolling across the water,
    crashing against the rocks,
    breaking upon the shore;
    day after day the same –
    the tide coming in, going out,
    in a never-ending cycle,
    a constant battle between land and sea.
And it felt to me that my life is like that,
    so much movement,
    so much effort,
    but achieving what?
I've tried my best, Lord,
    struggling for so long to achieve something,
    but where has it got me?
I wonder sometimes,
    for I'm the same person I always was,
    facing the same obstacles,

dreaming the same dreams
and fighting the same battles.
It's hard, Lord, to keep on going,
  to find the energy and enthusiasm to try again
  when all my efforts have been in vain –
  another day at the office,
  another hundred miles on the clock,
  another ream of paper,
  and still I've barely scratched the surface.
It was different once,
  when I was young,
  idealism then refusing to be denied,
  hope springing eternal;
  but now, when I stop to measure all I've done,
  I see one step forward and another back,
  an endless road to nowhere.

My child,
  I hear what you're saying,
  and I understand,
  for I feel it myself sometimes,
  even me.
It *is* hard when all your efforts are frustrated,
  when you give everything and it comes to nothing;
  and there will be moments
  when you feel like giving up,
  your time seeming wasted and your work in vain.
But it's then most of all that you need to keep striving,
  to battle on against the odds,
  for though you may not see it,

results are there –
imperceptible perhaps,
unrecognised,
but little by little taking shape,
slowly coming to fruition.
Take heart, my child,
and keep going,
for so often it's when you least expect it,
and where you last might think to look,
that dawn breaks and daylight comes.

*We are afflicted in every way, but not crushed;
perplexed, but not driven to despair; persecuted, but not forsaken; struck down, but not
destroyed . . . because we know that the one
who raised the Lord Jesus will raise us also
with Jesus, and will bring us with you into his
presence. So we do not lose heart. Even
though our outer nature is wasting away, our
inner nature is being renewed day by day. For
this slight momentary affliction is preparing us
for an eternal weight of glory beyond all
measure, because we look not at what can be
seen but at what cannot be seen; for what can
be seen is temporary, but what cannot be seen
is eternal.* 2 Corinthians 4:8-9, 14, 16-18

*Do not abandon that confidence of yours; it
brings a great reward. For you need endurance,
so that when you have done the will of God,*

you may receive what was promised. We are not among those who shrink back and so are lost, but among those who have faith and so are saved. Now faith is the assurance of things hoped for, the conviction of things not seen.

Hebrews 10:35-36, 39; 11:1

40

It was the simplest of sounds

One of the things people crave most in our modern world, but find hardest to obtain, is the gift of peace. Our lives are filled with noise – the roar of traffic in our streets; the clatter of machinery at the factory; the buzz of computers, telephones and fax machines in the office; the blaring of radios, televisions and hi-fi systems at home – all this and so much more adds up to a daily bombardment of sound. Quietness is a luxury, so rarely encountered that some people find it disconcerting, even intimidating. Yet silence offers a unique time to reflect, a time to commune with our own soul and be still before God. It is not that we cannot discover God equally in the noisy bustle of life, for of course we can, but a few moments' silence away from it all can help us rediscover a sense of inner tranquillity, a glimpse of that peace the Apostle Paul speaks of which passes all understanding.

The Lord is my shepherd, I shall not want. He makes me lie down in green pastures; he leads me beside still waters; he restores my soul. He leads me in right paths for his name's sake.

Psalm 23:1-3

Peace I leave with you; my peace I give to you. I do not give to you as the world gives. Do not let your hearts be troubled, and do not let them be afraid. John 14:27

It was the simplest of sounds –
    the song of a skylark high in the sky –
    but to me, Lord, it was the song of an angel,
    a harbinger of peace.
I stood and listened, spellbound,
    transported to another world,
    for in that joyful music,
    those innocent notes,
    there came back memories
    of carefree days and tranquil moments,
    of life untouched by the endless quest for gain.
And I rejoiced, Lord, in the beauty of it all,
    savouring the magic of that moment –
    my thoughts still,
    my mind calm,
    my soul at rest.
I realised then how I needed that moment,
    for I'd lost sight of self,
    of life,
    of you –
    but suddenly I saw again
    the nagging fears and hidden doubts,
    the crowding concerns and frantic haste,
    all put into perspective
    beside the things that really count,

and I wanted simply to stay, Lord,
lest the spell be broken,
and peace be lost.

My child,
you *did* need that time, just as you say –
those quiet few moments
to hear again my still small voice –
but if you were afraid to let go in case you lost me,
scared to move on in case you fell back,
then either you didn't get the message
or you failed to hear it all.
For the peace I offer is not just a fleeting thing,
here today and gone tomorrow;
it's an inner serenity that will not be shaken,
a calmness of spirit in the fiercest of storms.
Don't try to make sense of it,
for it's beyond expression,
unlike anything the world can give;
for even in the most troubled of moments,
and most hectic of days,
you will find stillness of mind
and rest for your soul.
So come to me now, and let my love enfold you;
then turn around and go in peace.

*I will both lie down and sleep in peace; for you
alone, O Lord, make me lie down in safety.*
Psalm 4:8

Peace be to you, and peace be to your house, and peace be to all that you have.

1 Samuel 25:6

Now may the Lord of peace himself give you peace at all times in all ways.

2 Thessalonians 3:16

Do not worry about anything, but in everything by prayer and supplication with thanksgiving let your requests be made known to God. And the peace of God, which surpasses all understanding, will guard your hearts and your minds in Christ Jesus. Philippians 4:6-7

_____41_____

I'm getting older

There comes a time in our lives, sooner or later, when it dawns on us that we are not as young as we used to be. Whereas the future once seemed to stretch out in front of us indefinitely, suddenly it seems all too short, the time left to us, to do all the things we once dreamed of doing, far less than we thought. To be confronted with that truth is profoundly painful, yet we cannot avoid it, however hard we try to hang on to the last vestiges of our youth. Time and tide, as they say, wait for no man. Yet, in the context of faith, the passage of time should not be seen as the years running out so much as life moving on, one more step along an unfolding journey in which there is always more to be discovered and new joys to be experienced. Of course, we will sometimes remember the past with a tinge of regret, and look ahead to the future with a degree of anxiety, but we shall also recognise each day as God's gift, and live each one of them in the assurance that nothing will ever separate us from his love made known in Christ.

Remember your Creator in the days of your youth, before the days of trouble come, and the years draw near when you will say, 'I have no *pleasure in them'; before the silver cord is snapped, and the golden bowl is broken, and the pitcher is broken at the fountain, and the wheel broken at the cistern, and the dust returns to the earth as it was, and the breath returns to God who gave it.*　　　Ecclesiastes 12:1, 6-7

Lord, let me know my end, and what is the measure of my days; let me know how fleeting my life is. You have made my days a few hand-breadths, and my lifetime is as nothing in your sight. Surely everyone stands as a mere breath. Surely everyone goes about like a shadow. Surely for nothing they are in turmoil; they heap up, and do not know who will gather.

Psalm 39:4-6

You turn us back to dust, and say, 'Turn back, you mortals.' Our years come to an end like a sigh. The days of our life are seventy years, or perhaps eighty, if we are strong; even then their span is only toil and trouble; they are soon gone, and we fly away.　　　Psalm 90:3, 9b-10

I'm getting older, Lord;
　　one by one the seconds are ticking past,
　　and the days drifting by.
I never noticed it before,
　　for life stretched out before me,
　　exciting,

rich with promise,
full of untold possibilities.
But now it's different,
for time has stolen up and caught me unawares,
and all of a sudden I find myself
looking back as much as forward,
yearning for bygone moments,
morbidly treading the aisles of memory
instead of anticipating new horizons.
I try to stop it,
frantically filling the present moment,
but before I know it a week has gone,
a month has passed,
a year is over.
Lord, I never realised how short life is,
how brief this fleeting span of ours,
but I see it now all too starkly,
and I'm troubled.
You see, I thought I would feel different,
that I would change in tandem with the years,
but I haven't,
and there's no sign I'm going to.
The hair may be thinner
and the brow more furrowed,
the limbs less supple and the energy diminished,
but I'm still the same person I always was –
a youngster looking out through ageing eyes.
Lord, I'm getting older,
and I don't like it,
I don't like it at all.

My child,
  don't be afraid,
  for there's joy as well as sorrow as the years go by.
Yes, it means time is passing,
  and there is pain in letting go and moving on.
Yes, there are memories mounting up
  one on the other,
  each of them precious, yet tinged with sadness.
And, yes, there is less time ahead of you
  than there used to be,
  the realisation of your mortality
  growing ever more stark
  and harder to bear.
But it's not in the past or the future you live –
  it's the present,
  the here and now.
You've glimpsed that truth but misunderstood it,
  turning it into threat instead of promise –
  a fact to dread instead of welcome.
Remember, my child, that each day is a gift,
  every moment within it needing to be lived
  as though it is your first and your last,
  for whether you are seven or seventy,
  young or old,
  there is always joy to discover,
  and blessing to find,
  beauty to glimpse,
  and love to share.
Each day I am with you,
  every step of your way,
  and when the journey is over

and the curtain falls,
I will still be with you,
taking your hand and leading you onwards –
what seemed the end, a new beginning,
another chapter,
where life will beckon for all eternity.

*The glory of youths is their strength, but the
beauty of the aged is their grey hair.*
Proverbs 20:29

*And now, O Lord, what do I wait for? My hope
is in you.*
Psalm 39:7

*Listen to me . . . all who have been borne by me
from your birth, carried from the womb; even to
your old age I am he, even when you turn grey I
will carry you. I have made, and I will bear; I will
carry and will save.*
Isaiah 46:3-4

42

It was only a fleeting glimpse

When did you last hear a sermon or a prayer on the theme of lust? Last week? Last month? I very much doubt it. There are some subjects we rarely air in church, and one of those is sex. A vital part of our lives it may be, but most people find it too embarrassing to talk about openly. The result is a mixture of guilt, misunderstanding and uncertainty in the minds of many as they struggle to come to terms with feelings of sexual attraction and even outright lust. It may be convenient to sweep such emotions under the carpet, but ultimately, like all else, they need to be brought honestly before God, if what was intended to be a special gift is not to be squandered in empty passion.

At the window of my house I looked out through my lattice, and I saw among the simple ones, I observed among the youths, a young man without sense, passing along the street near her corner, taking the road to her house in the twilight, in the evening, at the time of night and darkness. Then a woman comes towards him . . . she seizes and kisses him, and with impudent face she says to him: 'Come, let us take our fill of love until morning;

let us delight ourselves with love. For my
husband is not at home; he has gone on a long
journey.' Right away he follows her, and goes
like an ox to the slaughter, or bounds like a
stag toward the trap until an arrow pierces his
entrails. He is like a bird rushing into a snare,
not knowing that it will cost him his life.

Proverbs 7:6-10, 13, 18-19, 22-23

It was only a fleeting glimpse, Lord,
    a tantalising flash of naked flesh
    on the front of the newspaper,
    but it was enough,
    and I felt lust stir within.
It was wrong, I knew it,
    degrading both man and woman,
    yet despite myself it found a place,
    lurking in the shadows of my mind.
I turned away,
    thrusting the image aside,
    but it was still there,
    clamouring for attention,
    and I could not deny its hold.
Why, Lord?
Why can't I shut it out?
It's beyond sense and logic,
    an empty promise unable to satisfy,
    yet when I look inside I see my weakness,
    and fear my frailty.
It's you I blame rather than me.

Didn't you know the hurt you'd cause,
    the lives you'd wreck,
    the love you'd shatter,
    the dreams you'd crush,
    all for a moment's passion?
You tell us, Lord, that you want us to love,
    but, if so, why did you give us lust?

My child,
    it was a risk, I can't deny it,
    but isn't that true of every gift and every blessing?
There are always two sides:
    a good and a bad,
    a beautiful and an ugly,
    and the potential for either to win the day.
So don't be afraid of your feelings,
    or think them wrong;
    rather understand just how to show them.
I made you for love,
    the joyful joining of two lives,
    body and soul,
    flesh and spirit,
    the one complementing the other,
    each an expression of your whole being.
It's up to you, no one else –
    you can use or abuse what I have given,
    treasuring it as a jewel
    or squandering it as a trinket.
Divorce lust from love,
    and you may find instant pleasure,
    but never lasting joy.

Indulge your senses,
> and your flesh may be satisfied for a moment,
> but never your soul.

Remember, my child
> the choice is yours,
> but so also are the consequences.

Therefore a man leaves his father and his mother and clings to his wife, and they become one flesh. Genesis 2:24

He who commits adultery has no sense; he who does it destroys himself. He will get wounds and dishonour, and his disgrace will not be wiped away. Proverbs 6:32-33

Rejoice in the wife of your youth, a lovely deer, a graceful doe. May her breasts satisfy you at all times; may you be intoxicated always by her love. Why should you be intoxicated, my son, by another woman and embrace the bosom of an adulteress? Proverbs 5:18b-20

Shun fornication! Every sin that a person commits is outside the body; but the fornicator sins against the body itself. Or do you not know that your body is a temple of the Holy Spirit within you, which you have from God, and that you are not your own? For you were bought with a price; therefore glorify God in your body. 1 Corinthians 6:18-20

43

Why did it have to end?

The other morning I received a letter from the college where I trained for the ministry, informing me that after long debate and protracted negotiation a new building was to be bought and the old one sold off. Exciting news, we were told, paving the way for a fresh new chapter in the college's history. Only through this move could the training of Baptist ministers in Bristol be assured into the next millennium. And no doubt this was true. Yet for me, reading that letter, it was hard not to feel a pang of regret, for it meant that a place full of memory, brimming with nostalgia, would soon be changed for ever. Old memories would be wiped away as a new identity was stamped on that familiar and well-loved building. Yet that, of course, is so often true of life. Change is inevitable, and though it may bring pain and a sense of loss we must learn to welcome it.

These things I remember, as I pour out my soul: how I went with the throng and led them in procession to the house of God, with glad shouts and songs of thanksgiving, a multitude keeping festival. Psalm 42:4

*A voice says, 'Cry out!' And I said, 'What shall
I cry?' All people are grass, their constancy is
like the flower of the field. The grass withers,
the flower fades, when the breath of the Lord
blows upon it; surely the people are grass.*

Isaiah 40:6-7

Why did it have to end, Lord?
We'd worked so hard to reach that moment,
    to achieve something lasting and worthwhile,
    and life was good,
    as we'd always hoped it might be.
Not perfect, of course,
    for there were still problems to face
    and work to be done,
    but we were happy,
    at peace with ourselves,
    at one with the world.
And we gave our all,
    gladly,
    joyfully,
    wanting nothing,
    having everything.
I know I shouldn't indulge in nostalgia,
    but I can't help it, Lord,
    for it was the best time of my life,
    and I want to go back to the good old days,
    the way things used to be,
    for I never realised at the time
    how special those days were,

or how much they meant.
I do now, though – all too clearly –
   and my heart aches with the memories –
   the moments we shared,
   the people we knew,
   the pleasure we gave,
   the joy we received.
It was good, Lord,
   a precious, priceless time –
   why did it have to end?

My child,
   there's nothing wrong with nostalgia –
   never think that.
You've experienced much,
   and it's right to recall it,
   to reflect on the good times,
   to remember the past.
But to try to *live* there, that *would* be wrong –
   a squandering of the past and denial of the future,
   for what's here today is gone tomorrow,
   what one moment is certain
   the next may be shaken.
You're surrounded by change,
   each moment,
   each day;
   nothing, however precious,
   however solid,
   safe from the passage of time.
Nothing, that is, except my word,

my purpose,
and my love.
It's in these you must put trust,
where hope alone must rest,
for though heaven and earth may pass away
these will never change.
Look back with thanks,
look forward with hope,
remember the past,
reach out for the future –
for I offer love which endures for ever,
and joy that will never end,
in this life, or the next.

*The grass withers, the flower fades; but the word
of our God will stand for ever.*   Isaiah 40:8

I the Lord do not change.   Malachi 3:6

*Heaven and earth will pass away, but my words
will not pass away.*   Luke 21:33

*'What no eye has seen, nor ear heard, nor the
human heart conceived, what God has prepared for those who love him' – these things
God has revealed to us through the Spirit.*
1 Corinthians 2:9-10a

*Jesus Christ is the same yesterday and today
and for ever.*   Hebrews 13:8

___44___

I did it, Lord!

'I can't do it.' How often have you made that excuse when faced with a difficult and demanding challenge? Just occasionally it may be justified, but more often than not the truth is that we either don't want to do what's asked of us or fear we may make a fool of ourselves if we attempt it. The task in question may well be within our capabilities, but we would rather not risk finding out, just in case. Yet, unless we are prepared to face such situations head on, unless we are ready to have a go, never mind the consequences, we will never realise our true potential, constantly held back by half-formed fears and uncertainties. Two old sayings make the point well – 'Nothing ventured, nothing gained' and 'Nothing succeeds like success.'

I can do all things through him who strengthens me.   Philippians 4:13

I did it, Lord!
I never thought I would,
    never thought I had it in me,
    but I did,
    and it feels wonderful.

It was a near thing, though,
    many the time I felt like giving up,
    for it seemed too difficult,
    way beyond my capabilities,
    and I don't mind admitting
    the very idea filled me with dread.
It haunted me –
    there when I woke up, eating away inside,
    there at night, disturbing my sleep,
    there in the day, leering from the shadows –
    and I wanted to run from the challenge,
    to push it aside and curl up in safety.
It just wasn't me, I told myself –
    let someone else take it on –
    but there was no escape,
    for I knew if I passed the moment by
    it might never return,
    the chance gone,
    the opportunity wasted.
So I stuck with it, Lord,
    the fear growing,
    the panic mounting,
    yet determined to give my best.
And I did it –
    when the time came,
    and the moment arrived,
    I did it!

My child,
    of course you did it!
I knew you would.
You may have doubted yourself,
    but I didn't, never for a moment.
How could I, when I made you,
    fashioning you with my own hands?
I know what you're capable of,
    the heights you can reach,
    and, believe me, you've barely started yet,
    the world at your fingertips,
    the sky the limit.
Yes, you have your weaknesses like anyone else –
    the things you can't do,
    the things you do badly –
    but whoever you are,
    and however you may feel,
    they're as nothing beside your strengths.
If that's true *without* me,
    it's all the more so *with* me –
    if I'm by your side no challenge is beyond you,
    no task too hard.
Where you are weak, I am strong,
    where you have doubt, I bring faith,
    where you see problems, I give answers.
So keep going, my child,
    believe in yourself and believe in me.
You've tackled one hurdle;
    now face the rest.

Someone from the crowd answered him, 'Teacher, I brought you my son; he has a spirit that makes him unable to speak . . . if you are able to do anything, have pity on us and help us.' Jesus said to him, 'If you are able! – All things can be done for the one who believes.'

Mark 9:17, 22b-23

Nothing will be impossible with God.

Luke 1:37

My grace is sufficient for you, for power is made perfect in weakness. 2 Corinthians 12:9

45

I still can't believe it

There can be no experience more devastating than the loss of a loved one. However much we think we are prepared for it, when bereavement comes it sweeps over us, sucking us into a vortex of numbness and despair. The intensity and duration of emotional turmoil involved can be frightening, both to the person bereaved and those who seek to comfort them. Yet there are no easy words to offer, nor is there any right way to cope – everybody comes to terms with death in their own way and at their own pace. Grief needs to be expressed or it will slowly poison within. But the pain of bereavement will never be entirely removed; at best it can be made easier to bear. God understands that most of all.

The king said to the Cushite, 'Is it well with the young man Absalom?' The Cushite answered, 'May the enemies of my lord the king, and all who rise up to do you harm, be like that young man.' The king was deeply moved, and went up to the chamber over the gate and wept; and as he went, he said, 'O my son Absalom, my son, my son Absalom! Would that I had died instead of you, Absalom, my son, my son!' 2 Samuel 18:32-33

*When Mary came where Jesus was and saw
him, she knelt at his feet and said to him, 'Lord,
if you had been here, my brother would not
have died.' When Jesus saw her weeping, and
the Jews who came with her also weeping, he
was greatly disturbed in spirit and deeply
moved. He said, 'Where have you laid him?'
They said to him, 'Lord, come and see.' Jesus
began to weep. So the Jews said, 'See how he
loved him!' But some of them said, 'Could not
he who opened the eyes of the blind man have
kept this man from dying?'*   John 11:32-37

I still can't believe it, Lord –
    to think that after all we shared together,
    everything we went through,
    I will never see her again.
It doesn't seem possible,
    for she was always so full of life,
    brimming over with happiness,
    bubbling with enthusiasm.
Yet there's no denying it,
    for I saw her lying there,
    the body cold,
    the life gone.
It's over Lord, I realise that,
    but it all seems so unreal,
    like some ghastly dream,
    some grotesque joke;
    and although my mind accepts what's happened,

my heart says otherwise:
still listening for the sound of her voice,
still longing for the touch of her hand,
still searching for a glimpse of her face.
It will pass, so they tell me –
in time the wounds will heal
and the dull ache start to ease.
One day I will look at her photograph
not with numbness but with thanksgiving;
I will speak her name
not with tears of sorrow but tears of joy;
and I will look back remembering all that was
instead of all that might have been.
So at least they tell me, Lord,
and I know they mean well –
after all, life must go on.
Yet I don't want it to, not any more,
for I'm alone now,
my loved one plucked from me –
and I still can't believe it.

My child,
what can I say?
For I know no words can ease your pain,
or fill the emptiness.
But you're not alone,
for I am with you in the darkness,
reaching out to touch your bruised
and battered soul.
It hurts – of course it does –

and it will go on hurting, desperately,
day after day,
year after year,
until your final breath.
You'll never forget,
and never lose that sense of emptiness within,
for you have lost someone precious,
unique and irreplaceable in your life,
and not even time can smooth such pain away.
The wound may heal a little,
the scar become less livid,
but it will always be with you –
the price of joy,
the cost of love.
Yet I promise you this –
if you can greet your grief openly,
not letting it fester but meeting it face to face,
then you *will* find comfort,
rest for your soul;
and along with that, hope,
rising like a phoenix from the ashes,
stronger and deeper
than any you have known before –
a hope able to smile through the tears
and weep through the laughter,
knowing that I am there in both.
Believe me, my child, the time will come
when you will meet your loved one again,
united with her and me and all my people
in a new and glorious kingdom,
where there will be no more pain or sorrow,

no more tears or darkness,
but life in all its fullness,
life which will never end.

Blessed are those who mourn, for they will be comforted. Matthew 5:4

Jesus said to her, 'Your brother will rise again.' Martha said to him, 'I know that he will rise again in the resurrection on the last day.' Jesus said to her, 'I am the resurrection and the life. Those who believe in me, even though they die, will live, and everyone who lives and believes in me will never die. Do you believe this?' She said to him, 'Yes, Lord, I believe that you are the Messiah, the Son of God, the one coming into the world.' John 11:23-27

Then I saw a new heaven and a new earth; for the first heaven and the first earth had passed away, and the sea was no more. And I saw the holy city, the new Jerusalem, coming down out of heaven from God, like a bride adorned for her husband. And I heard a loud voice from the throne saying, 'See, the home of God is among mortals. He will dwell with them; they will be his peoples, and God himself will be with them; he will wipe away every tear from their eyes. Death will be no more; mourning and crying and pain will be no

more, for the first things have passed away.'
There will be no more night; they need no light
of lamp or sun, for the Lord God will be their
light, and they will reign for ever and ever.
Revelation 21:1-4; 22:5

__46__

I'm looking

There's a pithy little saying often displayed around Christmas time perhaps on a church notice board or car windscreen. The words? 'Wise men still seek him!' And of course it's true, for there are many today, just as there have always been, who still search in vain to find faith. It's not that they don't want to believe – quite the opposite – but there is so much in the world they cannot make sense of, so much which seems to contradict the God of love preached by the Christian faith. Yet, paradoxically, it is precisely here, in all the need and complexity of this world, rather than in some distant vision of heaven, that all of us need to look for answers, for unless faith speaks to our human situation now, it is worthless. It's not just wise men who need to remember that – it's all of us!

When you search for me, you will find me; if you seek me with all your heart, I will let you find me, says the Lord.   Jeremiah 29:13-14a

Thomas said to him, 'Lord, we do not know where you are going. How can we know the way?'   John 14:5

I'm looking Lord,
    looking to make sense of this bleeding,
    broken world of ours,
    looking to find you in the mystery of it all,
    to grab hold of something
    that will give purpose, meaning,
    direction to my life.
No, I'm not just looking,
    I'm searching –
    eagerly,
    hungrily,
    desperately –
    needing to find some answers,
    needing to find you!
For if I'm honest, Lord –
    really honest for a change –
    I'm just drifting along,
    muddling through from one day to the next,
    pretending I have it sorted,
    appearing to be in control;
    but in reality simply getting by as best I can.
And deep down I'm hungry,
    thirsty,
    longing to be filled,
    to satisfy that nagging, gnawing pain within me
    which nothing seems to ease.
Lord, I'm looking,
    I'm searching,
    I'm begging –
    help!

My child,
>   you are looking, I can see that,
>   but I'm not sure why,
>   for I've told you what I want,
>   told you where to find me –
>   so what's the problem?
I've been calling you constantly –
>   day after day,
>   week after week,
>   year after year –
>   haven't you been listening?
That was me, just now, shouting your name,
>   in the cry of the hungry,
>   the groan of the oppressed,
>   the anger of the poor,
>   the plight of the needy.
That was me in the hurt of the orphan,
>   the despair of the homeless,
>   the frustration of the unemployed,
>   the sorrow of the outcast.
That was me in the darkness of the depressed,
>   the tears of the lonely,
>   the fear of the weak,
>   and the pain of the sick.
I've been beating at your door,
>   asking incessantly for admittance,
>   looking for just a little space
>   in that crowded life of yours,
>   but there's been no room,
>   never any time for anyone but yourself.
Oh yes, you've looked for me, I grant you that –

I saw you in church the other day,
and heard your prayer – don't question that.
But you've got things wrong,
   turned faith around,
   too preoccupied with the trees to see the wood.
You talk of making sense of this messy world,
   but I'm telling you,
   unless you can find me somewhere in it,
   and unless you can help to make me real there,
   then I'm sorry, but you'll go on looking,
   and go on searching as often as you like,
   yet never find me.

*If you close your ear to the cry of the poor,
you will cry out and not be heard.*

Proverbs 21:13

*When the Son of Man comes in his glory, and
all the angels with him, then he will sit on
the throne of his glory. All the nations will be
gathered before him, and he will separate
people one from another as a shepherd sepa-
rates the sheep from the goats, and he will put
the sheep at his right hand and the goats at
the left. Then the king will say to those at his
right hand, 'Come, you that are blessed by
my Father, inherit the kingdom prepared for
you from the foundation of the world; for I
was hungry and you gave me food, I was
thirsty and you gave me something to drink, I*

was a stranger and you welcomed me, I was naked and you gave me clothing, I was sick and you took care of me, I was in prison and you visited me.' Then the righteous will answer him, 'Lord, when was it that we saw you hungry and gave you food, or thirsty and gave you something to drink? And when was it that we saw you a stranger and welcomed you, or naked and gave you clothing? And when was it that we saw you sick or in prison and visited you?' And the king will answer them, 'Truly I tell you, just as you did it to one of the least of these who are members of my family, you did it to me.'   Matthew 25:31-40

47

God, I asked you to speak

Prayer, if we take it seriously, involves risks – the risk first that we may be disappointed by God's answer or lack of it, and the risk second that it may lead to more than we had bargained for. It may still be sometimes that, for all our efforts, God doesn't seem to answer, although I hope this collection of meditations may have suggested some possible ways in which he may be speaking. But it may also be that the answer he gives is somewhat different from the one we'd hoped for; that instead of soothing or reassuring it brings an awkward, disturbing challenge which we'd rather not hear. The question then, of course, is are we willing to listen, or do we close our ears? True prayer can be costly, yet it is also infinitely rewarding, for to experience the presence of God is to discover life itself, in all its mystery and wonder.

The word of God is living and active, sharper than any two-edged sword, piercing until it divides soul from spirit, joints from marrow; it is able to judge the thoughts and intentions of the heart. Hebrews 4:12

God, I asked you to speak,
    and you spoke,
    and I wish now I'd kept quiet,
    for your word is frightening,
    challenging,
    demanding,
    disturbing.
It breaks into my comfortable complacency,
    it upsets my quiet composure,
    it questions my willingness to compromise,
    it threatens my hard-won confidence.
God, I asked you to speak,
    and you spoke,
    and now I'm asking you to help me listen,
    help me accept,
    and help me to respond.

My child,
    it's come as a shock, hasn't it,
    this answer I've given?
But it shouldn't have done,
    not if your prayer was genuine.
You looked to me for guidance,
    and I gave it;
    not perhaps what you wanted to hear,
    nor what you expected,
    but what you asked for nonetheless –
    my word to you,
    searching,
    rebuking,
    renewing.

It's up to you now, what you make of it.
You can close your ears and turn away,
    pretending you never heard me,
    or in faith you can face my challenge
    and find light for your path,
    food for your soul,
    the word that offers life.

My beloved child, continue in what you have learned and firmly believed, knowing from whom you learned it, and how from childhood you have known the sacred writings that are able to instruct you for salvation through faith in Christ Jesus. All scripture is inspired by God and is useful for teaching, for reproof, for correction, and for training in righteousness, so that everyone who belongs to God may be proficient, equipped for every good work.
2 Timothy 1:2a; 3:14-17

Thematic Index

The references are to meditations rather than page numbers.